CLASSICS IN
Lawrence A. Cremin

☆ ☆ ☆

THE REPUBLIC AND THE SCHOOL
Horace Mann on the Education of Free Men
Edited by Lawrence A. Cremin

AMERICAN IDEAS ABOUT ADULT EDUCATION
1710–1951
Edited by C. Hartley Grattan

DEWEY ON EDUCATION
Introduction and Notes by Martin S. Dworkin

THE SUPREME COURT AND EDUCATION
Edited by David Fellman

INTERNATIONAL EDUCATION
A Documentary History
Edited by David G. Scanlon

CRUSADE AGAINST IGNORANCE
Thomas Jefferson on Education
Edited by Gordon C. Lee

CHINESE EDUCATION UNDER COMMUNISM
Edited by Chang-Tu Hu

CHARLES W. ELIOT AND POPULAR EDUCATION
Edited by Edward A. Krug

WILLIAM T. HARRIS ON EDUCATION
(in preparation)
Edited by Martin S. Dworkin

THE *EMILE* OF JEAN JACQUES ROUSSEAU
Selections
Translated and Edited by William Boyd

John Locke
on Education

Edited, with an Introduction and Notes, by
PETER GAY

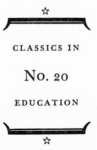

CLASSICS IN

No. 20

EDUCATION

BUREAU OF PUBLICATIONS
TEACHERS COLLEGE, COLUMBIA UNIVERSITY
NEW YORK

© 1964 by Peter Gay

Library of Congress Catalog Card
Number 64-14307

Printed in the United States of America
by the William Byrd Press, Inc.
Richmond, Virginia

Preface

One can turn to several of John Locke's essays for his views on education: the *Conduct of the Understanding,* the *Thoughts Concerning Reading and Study for a Gentleman,* or, indeed, the vastly different memorandum on working schools. But certainly *Some Thoughts Concerning Education* is his most significant and influential pedagogical treatise. The work belongs to the period of Locke's Dutch exile, the years between 1683 and 1689, during which he devoted himself primarily to the composition of his *Essay Concerning Human Understanding.* The *Thoughts* took form in a series of letters to Edward Clarke on the upbringing and education of Clarke's children; and indeed, there is no evidence that Locke originally contemplated publication. The correspondence did attract attention, however, for on March 2, 1693, Locke's friend William Molyneux wrote him from Dublin: "My brother has sometimes told me that whilst he had the happiness of your acquaintance at Leyden you were upon a work on the method of learning, and that, too, at the request of a tender father for the use of his only son. Wherefore, good sir, let me most earnestly entreat you by no means to lay aside this infinitely useful work till you have finished it, for 'twill be of vast advantage to all mankind, as well as particularly to me, your entire friend. . . ." Locke replied on March 28: "These letters, or at least some of them, have been seen by some of my acquaintance here, who would needs persuade me 'twould be of use to publish them. Your impatience to see them has not, I

assure you, slackened my hand or kept me in suspense."
Shortly thereafter, the work appeared.

Owing to their origin, the *Thoughts* are repetitive and
loosely organized, and Locke seems not to have perceived
them as systematically related to the doctrines he was
expounding in the *Essay*. Yet Professor Gay is quite
correct in arguing, contrary to earlier writers such as
Laurie, the inextricable connection between the two
works. Taken together, they were pivotal in the development of modern educational theory. They pro-
foundly influenced Rousseau, Kant, Basedow, and Pesta-
lozzi; and as Merle Curti has indicated, they were widely
known in the American colonies, not only in their original form, but through the popularizations of Benjamin
Franklin, Enos Hitchcock, Mrs. Louisa Hoare, and Isaac
Watts.

Professor Gay's argument for the continuing relevance
of Locke is equally well taken. As Herbert Quick re-
marked more than fifty years ago, Locke was no evange-
list, conscious of a mission to renovate the human race
through some grand educational discovery, but rather a
man of calm good sense, setting down the wisdom he had
gleaned during his years as physician, tutor, and man of
affairs. Balance, moderation, and practicality—these are
the qualities that mark *Some Thoughts Concerning Education*. The work stands in refreshing contrast to the
steady procession of utopias that constitute so much of
the heritage of Western educational thought.

LAWRENCE A. CREMIN

John Locke
on Education

Introduction

By PETER GAY

John Locke was the father of the Enlightenment in educational thought as in so much else. His *Essay Concerning
Human Understanding,* the product of prolonged reflection and several drafts, appeared in 1690 and laid the
psychological groundwork for modern educational theory.
His *Some Thoughts Concerning Education,* which took
coherent shape while he was writing and rewriting the
Essay, appeared three years later, in 1693, and applied
his philosophy specifically to pedagogy. These two books
rapidly became, and have remained, classics of modern
philosophy.

Like many another revolutionary, John Locke was also
a conservative, at once transmitting and transforming
traditional ideas. His treatise on education stands at the
beginning of the long cycle of modernity, but it stands,
too, at the end, and as the climax, of a long evolution—
the discovery of the child. During the Middle Ages, and
during the Renaissance, adults treated children as toys,
strange animals, or small grownups. Children mixed
readily in adult company, played infantile adaptations of
adult games, dressed in cut-down versions of adult clothing, overheard the grossest sexual allusions, and partici-
pated in overt sexual play. The precise age of the child
was unknown and, if known, irrelevant: the educational
process knew nothing of our automatic allocation of chil-

1

dren to classes or grades. Most children, of course, remained illiterate; but even among the educated, some began their schooling early, others late; some were confided to tutors at home, while others went away to school; some completed their education in three years, others in ten. Educators had little if any conception of the gradual evolution of rationality and self-discipline in the growing child or of the orderly development of subject matter. To the extent that children were important at all, their importance was economic and legal: they were sources of labor and links in the chain of inheritance.[1]

One reason for this casual treatment of children was their uncertain life expectancy. Even princes faced death with monotonous and dreadful regularity. In the Middle Ages, and in the Renaissance, too, men aged quickly and died young, but the most frequent victims of epidemics, vile nourishment, and misplaced medical care were young children.[2] Montaigne, a cool but not a cruel man, could record in his *Essais:* "I have lost two or three children in their infancy, not without regret, but without great grief";[3] and even in Locke's time, and after, a child's survival was so problematical that parents usually covered their losses in advance, by refusing to invest too much emotion in their offspring. Yet it seems likely that by the eighteenth century, if not before, most parents could remember just how many of their children they had lost, even if they could not muster the kind of grief we would now consider appropriate to such a tragic occasion. In

[1] See Philippe Ariès, *Centuries of Childhood,* translated by R. Baldick (New York, 1963).

[2] See Marc Bloch, *La société féodale: La formation des liens de dépendance* (Paris, 1939), pp. 116–120.

[3] This statement appears in "Of the Affection of Fathers for Their Children," Book II, Essay 8.

the 1750's, Rousseau abandoned his five illegitimate children, but when he confessed this later, he was exact about their number.[4]

Locke was both an expression and a cause of this shift in sensibility. The sixteenth and seventeenth centuries saw the growing rationalization of the world. There was a new calendar; there were mechanical clocks, improved administrative techniques (if only for the purpose of collecting taxes and suppressing dissent), and energetic inquiries into the sources and nature of knowledge. There were, above all, the magnificent, cumulative discoveries of "new philosophy." These changes were expressed in new kinds of schools, in which students were carefully differentiated by grades and guided by thoughtfully worked-out programs of study. But bold as they were, these academies and *collèges* had grave flaws; as everyone knows, it is rare that the moral and psychological possibilities suggested by new discoveries are fully embodied in social institutions. When Locke wrote *Some Thoughts Concerning Education,* most children remained beyond the pale of literacy, the schools then in existence taught by rote and disciplined with brutality, and the very understanding of childhood as a reputable phase in the life cycle remained the property of a few. It took books like Locke's and a half-century of insistent propaganda to diffuse the notion that children are human, with their own rights, their own rhythm of development, and their own pedagogical needs.

It has been argued that Locke owed much to the educational writings of Rabelais and Montaigne. The argu-

[4] See Jean-Jacques Rousseau, *Confessions,* in *Œuvres complètes* (Pléiade ed.; Paris, 1959–), I, 344–358. The extensive literature on this incident is analyzed *ibid.,* pp. 1416–1422.

ment is plausible, especially for Montaigne, who for all
his detachment could recognize that the games of children
deserve to be taken seriously and that compulsion is a
poor inducement to real learning. Yet in stressing the
crucial significance of education for the total physical
and psychic economy of the human being, Locke was the
true innovator. Montaigne did not, and could not, write,
as Locke did, that "of all the men we meet with, nine
parts of ten are what they are, good or evil, useful or not,
by their education. It is that which makes the great difference in mankind. The little, or almost insensible, impressions on our tender infancies, have very important
and lasting consequences." [5] Children, Locke goes on, are
like the fountains of rivers, which may be directed in
various courses by "a gentle application of the hand." [6]
This view is radical enough, although coupled with an
authoritarian cast of mind, it might amount to little more
than an injunction to manipulate pliant young minds.
But in Locke the claim for the strategic importance of
education was accompanied by a humane respect for the
child himself: *"Maxima debetur pueris reverentia,"* Locke
writes, quoting Juvenal—"the greatest respect is owed
to boys." [7] Indeed, Locke insists that grownups must respect children's "innocent folly, playing, and childish
actions" and leave them "perfectly free and unrestrained,"
for their faults are "faults of their age." [8] It is the temper
of these remarks, elaborated in paragraph after paragraph
of his *Thoughts,* that makes Locke most congenial to us,
and that made him the father of the Enlightenment in
educational thought.

[5] *Some Thoughts Concerning Education,* § 1.
[6] *Ibid.*
[7] *Ibid.,* § 71. The quotation is from Juvenal *Satires* xiv. 47.
[8] *Some Thoughts Concerning Education,* § 63.

II

The main reason for the immediate, and lasting, popularity of Locke's pedagogic writings was their intimate and obvious connection with his philosophy, a philosophy that came to dominate the eighteenth century. Like every true philosopher of education, Locke developed his pedagogical program, not in isolation, but as part of a total view of the world. It was as a philosopher that Locke the educator appealed to experience, expressed confidence in the flexibility of human nature, regarded human beings as organisms of interacting psychological and physical characteristics, and advocated humane treatment and utilitarian training.

It is a commonplace that Locke was an empiricist, but the far-reaching implications of his position have not always been recognized. By insisting on empiricism, Locke imported Newton's scientific method into philosophy and repudiated the great rationalist systems of his own century. He was among the first to advocate what his disciples, the eighteenth-century *philosophes,* would call "philosophical modesty." As he himself described his philosophical vocation, it was his task to inquire into the origins, certainty, and extent of human knowledge. This means that his inquiry was as much into the limitations as into the possibilities of knowledge. Indeed, he claims in a celebrated passage of his Introduction to the *Essay Concerning Human Understanding* that he is not writing philosophy at all. While his age, he writes, has such "master-builders" as Boyle and Sydenham and Huygens and "the incomparable Mr. Newton," he himself thought it "ambition enough to be employed as an under-labourer in clearing ground a little and removing some of the rubbish that lies in the way to knowledge."

When Locke uses such disparaging language about himself, he is attacking other philosophers, if only by implica-
tion. Much speculation, he suggests, is frivolous and pre-
tentious argument over words, or boastful system-making.
It is true, as he also argues in the Introduction to the
Essay, that "men have reason to be well satisfied with
what God hath thought fit for them," since they can
know "whatsoever is necessary for the conveniences of life
and information of virtue," but they know what they *can*
know through experience rather than dogma, by making
observations rather than syllogisms.

This rejection of dogmatism pervades Locke's *Thoughts
Concerning Education.* The book is by nature didactic,
but its many rules are based on experience. They suggest
that Locke had watched the children he knew with open
and benign eyes. Moreover, Locke's educational program
was not a divine pattern or a moral improbability, but a
sensible, attainable reality: it aimed to produce the civic-
minded, well-mannered, and soundly informed English
gentleman.

Nor is this all. Locke did not go as far as Rousseau was
to go in recommending an education that concentrated
first on experience and only later on reading, but his concern with exposing the child to life as well as to books
is remarkable for his time. Children understand reasoning
early and take pride in "being treated as rational creatures"; yet, Locke warns, "when I talk of reasoning, I do
not intend any other, but such as is suited to the child's
capacity and apprehension. Nobody can think a boy of
three or seven years old, should be argued with, as a
grown man. Long discourses, and philosophical reasonings, at best, amaze and confound, but do not instruct
children." [9] This piece of advice sounds much like

[9] *Ibid.,* § 81.

Rousseau's *Émile*. So does Locke's admonition to show young children pictures and objects to accompany their reading.[10]

Beyond this, Locke recognizes that education is not confined to formal exercises, but goes on in all transactions between adults and children, and among children themselves. That is why the *Thoughts Concerning Education* deals with the child's total environment. It warns against intimate commerce with servants, encourages children to study—and profit from—the art of conversation, and urges the inculcation of good habits through practice: "Pray remember, children are not to be taught by rules, which will be always slipping out of their memories. What you think necessary for them to do, settle in them by an indispensable practice, as often as the occasion returns; and, if it be possible, make occasions." [11] Since children learn by imitation, they must be given experiences worth imitating.

This sort of pragmatic empiricism is closely tied to Locke's doctrine that man's nature is receptive and malleable, especially in early youth. Locke devoted the entire first book of his *Essay Concerning Human Understanding* to a celebrated attack on the doctrine of "innate principles." The precise target of his long polemic remains a matter of discussion, but its consequences are plain.[12] Locke does not deny the existence of intuition. Nor does he deny the presence of innate capacities. He does deny that men have authoritative knowledge of such important matters as God, apart from experience

[10] See *ibid.*, § 156.

[11] *Ibid.*, § 66.

[12] In his authoritative *John Locke* (2nd ed.; Oxford, 1955), Richard I. Aaron defends the traditional view that Book I of Locke's *Essay* is directed primarily against Descartes and the Cartesians, as well as against some minor English thinkers who also held the doctrine of innate ideas.

and reflection on that experience; he affirms, conversely, that the environment exercises a pervasive power over men's minds.

The relevance of this view to education is obvious. To be sure, Locke, always moderate, concedes that "God has stamped certain characters upon men's minds, which, like their shapes, may perhaps be a little mended; but can hardly be totally altered and transformed into the contrary." [13] The good teacher does not try to force grave children to become gay and gay children to become grave, for "what is so plaistered on will at best sit but untowardly." [14] Yet if, as Locke says in the *Essay*, the child's mind at birth is like "white paper, void of all characters," [15] skillful educators may develop their pupil's "natural genius" to its limit. Here, as elsewhere, Locke's sensible restraint is typical of what is best in the thought of the Enlightenment; in the middle of the eighteenth century uncompromising environmentalists like Helvétius were to argue that men might learn almost anything and that cultures might thus be improved beyond all recognition in a few generations. So extreme a hope is not to be found in Locke, as it is not to be found in his best disciples, in Hume or in Voltaire.

One reason for Locke's moderation was that he saw the child's mind embedded in his total organism. As a physician, Locke begins his *Thoughts Concerning Education* with a quotation from Juvenal—"a sound mind in a sound body"—and continues with thirty paragraphs on the child's health, his food, his clothing, his exposure to air, all the way down to his bowel movements: "Plenty

---

13 *Some Thoughts Concerning Education*, § 66.
14 *Ibid*.
15 See *Essay Concerning Human Understanding*, Book II, Chapter 1.

of open air, exercise, and sleep; plain diet, no wine or strong drink, and very little or no physic; not too warm and strait clothing; especially the head and feet kept cold, and the feet often used to cold water and exposed to wet." [16] It is only after Locke has given a good deal of this sort of advice on hygiene that he is ready to embark on a discussion of how to train the mind.

This was a bold step for Locke to take; even if some of his advice would make today's physicians, or parents, wince, his recognition that mental development is related to physical condition is thoroughly modern. It was this recognition, too, that permitted him to understand the relation between motivation and learning. A listless and dreamy child must not be forced to learn, for he will only forget what he has learned, and quickly, too. On the contrary, the teacher must awaken the child's natural appetite for experience by appealing to his ruling passions. "Where there is no desire," Locke writes, reasonably enough, "there will be no industry." [17] On this point Locke insisted over and over again. Compulsion, the prevailing method of training the young, is absurd. Children naturally enjoy "variety and freedom," [18] and they naturally "hate to be idle." [19] It follows that they will enjoy learning as soon as it is made enjoyable: "None of the things they are to learn should ever be made a burden to them, or imposed on them as a task." [20]

These words show Locke not merely as a physician; they also reveal a personal quality on which I have already touched: Locke was a humane man. Humanitarianism was a personal quality, but, like his empiricism,

[16] *Some Thoughts Concerning Education*, § 30.
[17] *Ibid.*, § 126.
[18] *Ibid.*, § 128.
[19] *Ibid.*, § 129.
[20] *Ibid.*, § 73.

it was also part of his general philosophy, and his legacy to the dawning Enlightenment. The idea that individuals are precious pervades Locke's thought. His political liberalism teaches that the state is the agent rather than the master of the individual; his theory of toleration teaches that opinion, even erroneous opinion, has its value and should be heard. In politics, as in education, it is repression, not liberty, that breeds the cancer of sullen rebellion.[21] Just as the individual exists, not for the state, but for himself, so the child is neither the slave nor the plaything of adults, but a human being with his own worth.

This does not mean that Locke advocated the relaxation of all discipline; he was not *that* modern. Rather, he insisted that children owe respect and obedience to their elders. He insisted, too, that all the wishes of children ought not to be granted, and that habits of self-denial should be inculcated early: "He that has not a mastery over his inclinations, he that knows not how to resist the importunity of present pleasure or pain, for the sake of what reason tells him is fit to be done, wants the true principle of virtue and industry, and is in danger never to be good for anything." [22] At the same time, Locke had

[21] *A Letter Concerning Toleration,* Locke's celebrated plea for liberal policies toward dissent, was first published in Latin and immediately translated into English in 1689. It is one of his finest works, as humane as it is cogent. Yet the toleration it advocates is incomplete: the intolerant and the subversive have no place in an ordered commonwealth, and two groups, Roman Catholics (who are agents of a foreign power) and atheists (whose word and oath no one can trust), are specifically excluded from Locke's good state. These exceptions may strike the twentieth-century reader as narrow-minded or even absurd, but what is most noteworthy about them is that they are made on political rather than religious or tribal grounds.

[22] *Some Thoughts Concerning Education,* § 45.

nothing but contempt for the accepted form of punishment—beating—which he called the "usual lazy and short way." [23] Beating a child has no educational function of any sort: it does not get at the roots of misbehavior; it fosters disgust with learning rather than pleasure in it; it encourages either blind rebellion or slavish obedience, both undesirable traits in children as in adults. By breaking the mind, Locke warns, one creates a "low-spirited, moped creature," [24] fit only to please foolish grownups by his unnatural silence or servile obedience. The child is father to the man: the boy whose spirit has been broken will grow up "an useless thing to himself and others." [25]

Kindliness, then, is desirable for its own sake; it is appropriate to the human dignity of the child as much as to the dignity of the adult. But Locke offers another justification for it: it works. Locke, in fact, is persistently concerned with the consequences of his recommendations in daily life, with the utility of his program. Indeed, a utilitarian streak colors his educational proposals in general. Here we encounter a strain in Locke's thinking typical of much liberal theorizing down to the nineteenth century: Locke is radical, but he is also embedded in his time. He wants reform, but not for all men. On the one hand, Locke was impatient with the educational practices of his day which produced, he thought, idle and empty-headed wastrels. Listing the qualities he wishes to see cultivated in children, he begins with virtue (by which he means a gentle but courageous religiosity free from both "superstition" and "enthusiasm") and continues with respect for truth; to these he adds wisdom and good breeding. Learning comes last, a placement to which he

[23] *Ibid.*, § 47.
[24] *Ibid.*, § 51.
[25] *Ibid.*

refers, a little self-consciously, as "strange in the mouth
of a bookish man." [26] But Locke knew what he was about:
"Learning must be had, but in the second place, as subservient only to greater qualities." [27] Let the pupil learn
English well and read his Bible; let him be taught
French. Latin, "absolutely necessary to a gentleman," [28]
comes later, contrary to accepted practice, which makes a
fetish of this dead language: "Can there be anything more
ridiculous than that a father should waste his own money,
and his son's time, in setting him to learn the Roman
language, when, at the same time, he designs him for a
trade, wherein he, having no use of Latin, fails not to
forget that little which he brought from school, and
which it is ten to one he abhors for the ill usage it
procured him?" [29] Latin is necessary for some, but not for
all; time-honored subjects like logic or Greek might well
be omitted; history, geography, and anatomy might well
be substituted for useless learning—in a word, the educational system should adjust itself to the needs of life. Are
not these notions (just a little philistine even in Locke's
pure diction) all too familiar in our own time?

But the very real affinity of Locke's radical notions
with our age of democratic education should not blind us
to their equally real distance from it. Locke was, after all,
addressing his little book on education to a gentleman, on
the subject of the education of that gentleman's son and
in the hope that other gentlemen would read it. It never
occurred to him that every child should be educated or
that all those to be educated should be educated alike.
Locke believed that until the school system was reformed,

[26] *Ibid.*, § 147.
[27] *Ibid.*
[28] *Ibid.*, § 163.
[29] *Ibid.*, § 164.

a gentleman ought to have his son trained at home by a tutor, and he devoted some lengthy paragraphs of his *Thoughts Concerning Education* to the proper qualifications of such a tutor. As for the poor, they do not appear in Locke's little book at all, and we have to gather his ideas from a document he wrote in 1697. In his capacity as a commissioner of trade and plantations, Locke drafted a plan for the revision of the Elizabethan Poor Law in light of the almost overwhelming problem of pauperism in England.[30] The increase of the poor, he wrote, meant an increase in the burden of local taxation designed to provide for them. One way out was to prevent their debauchery by closing down taverns; another was to compel beggars to do hard labor at soldier's pay. But the most burdensome question was the children. Here Locke suggested some drastic remedies, remedies which seem oddly out of place with his general humanitarianism and which demonstrate that to seventeenth-century thinkers, even to radicals, the poor were barely human: "If any boy or girl, under fourteen years of age, shall be found begging out of the parish where they dwell . . . they shall be sent to the next working school, there to be soundly whipped and kept at work till evening, so that they may be dismissed time enough to get to their place of abode that night." [31] Since most of the children of the poor lived in vicious idleness, Locke proposed that "working schools be set up in every parish, to which the children of all such as demand relief of the parish, above three and under fourteen years of age, whilst they live at home with their parents, and are not otherwise employed for their livelihood by the allowance of the overseers of the poor,

[30] Locke's proposals are reprinted in H. R. Fox Bourne, *A Life of John Locke* (2 vols.; New York, 1876), II, 337–391.
[31] *Ibid.*, p. 381.

shall be obliged to come." [32] This would give the mothers
liberty to work and the children better food than they
would obtain at home: "If . . . care be taken that they
have each of them their belly-full of bread daily at school,
they will be in no danger of famishing, but, on the contrary, they will be healthier and stronger than those who
are bred otherwise." [33] This diet, Locke thought, should
be supplemented "in cold weather, if it be thought need-
ful," with "a little warm water gruel." [34] Since the children would be earning their way with what they produced, Locke added thoughtfully, the education of paupers would cost the parish nothing. I need hardly point
out that these working schools did not offer such subjects
as French or Latin, but confined themselves to teaching
the little paupers such manual skills as "spinning or
knitting, or some other part of woollen manufacture"
and such edifying matters as "some sense of religion." [35]
That was all; those who counted needed a knowledge of
geography and French, some dancing ability, and much
skill in conversation, but the poor did not count—not yet.

III

From the perspective of our time, such proposals for the
lower orders seem repellent, and inconsistent with the
rest of Locke's liberal and humane program. But to see
Locke in this way is to be unhistorical: it is easy to forget
just how different the seventeenth century was from our
own. The lot of man was scarcity, not abundance; social

[32] *Ibid.,* p. 383.
[33] *Ibid.,* p. 384.
[34] *Ibid.*
[35] *Ibid.,* p. 385.

hierarchies remained steep and class divisions sharp. Egalitarian democracy in education would have seemed the wildest of Utopian dreams to men in Locke's time. Indeed, in his own day, Locke was denounced as a radical, in education as in religion, and it is significant that Rousseau's *Émile,* probably the most influential revolutionary tract on education that we have, shows Locke's influence on page after page. Therefore, if we seek the roots of what is valuable in modern educational philosophy, we must turn to Locke's *Thoughts Concerning Education,* even if many of its specific recommendations are now out of date or wholly irrelevant. And more: if we want to remind ourselves why we really wish to educate children, if we seek a philosophy that insists on the relevance of subject matter to experience without neglecting the pleasure of cultivation for its own sake, that emphasizes recognition of the child's needs without ignoring the uses of discipline, that urges the relation of morale to learning without denying the virtue of hard study, that seeks to form men and women fit for modern life without forgetting that this fitness requires cultivation of the higher sensibilities and a profound knowledge of the great literature of the past—if we seek such an educational theory we would do well to read, and reread, Locke with care.

SHORT BIBLIOGRAPHY

The most complete and most recent edition of Locke's works remains the ten-volume edition of 1823. Since the Lovelace collection of Locke's papers has now become available to scholars, several of his writings have appeared in critical editions. See, above all, Peter Laslett's brilliant

critical edition of the *Two Treatises of Government*
(Cambridge, England, 1960), which has an important in-
troduction; see also Wolfgang von Leyden's edition of
Locke's *Essays on the Laws of Nature* (Oxford, 1954) and
John Lough's edition of *Locke's Travels in France, As
Related in His Journals, Correspondence and Other
Papers* (Cambridge, England, 1953). For the Lovelace
papers, see P. Long, *A Summary Catalogue of the Love-
lace Collection of the Papers of John Locke in the
Bodleian Library* (Oxford, 1959).

The best general analysis of Locke's thought is Richard
I. Aaron, *John Locke* (2nd ed.; Oxford, 1955), which contains a full but selective bibliography of writings by and
about Locke. J. W. Yolton, *John Locke and the Way of
Ideas* (London, 1956) has much revealing material on the
reception of Locke's ideas by his pious contemporaries.
James Gibson, *Locke's Theory of Knowledge and Its His-
torical Relations* (Cambridge, England, 1917) is a techni-
cal study of Locke's epistemology which supplements
Aaron's work well. D. J. O'Connor's little Penguin volume, *John Locke* (Harmondsworth, England, 1952) is an
intelligent introduction.

Since Locke's political thought was of immense his-
torical significance, it has received much attention from
interpreters. J. W. Gough, *John Locke's Political Philosophy* (Oxford, 1950) is a sensible series of essays, which may
be contrasted with C. B. Macpherson's radical, stimulat-
ing reinterpretation, *The Political Theory of Possessive
Individualism: Hobbes to Locke* (Oxford, 1962). Ray-
mond Polin, *La politique morale de John Locke* (Paris,
1960) is a brilliant essay by a trained philosopher.

There is room for a comprehensive biography of Locke.
Fox Bourne's old *Life of John Locke* (2 vols.; New York,
1876) remains useful and is a full report on Locke's

career, but much new material has appeared since Fox Bourne wrote, and many of his opinions now seem dated. This new material has been used to good advantage by Maurice Cranston in his *John Locke, A Biography* (New York, 1957), a book much enlivened by its use of the Lovelace papers. Its treatment of Locke's ideas, however, is sketchy.

Locke's educational ideas are treated briefly by Aaron, but most books dealing with them at length are rather old. In addition to J. W. Adamson's edition of the *Thoughts,* see also his *Pioneers of Modern Education, 1600-1700* (Cambridge, England, 1905); F. A. Arnstädt, *François Rabelais und sein Traité d'Education mit besonderer Berücksichtigung der pädagogischen Grundsätze Montaignes, Lockes und Rousseaus* (Leipzig, 1872); Pierre Villey, *L'influence de Montaigne sur les idées pédagogiques de Locke et de Rousseau* (Paris, 1911); and the more recent study by Nina Reicyn, *La pédagogie de John Locke* (Paris, 1941).

Some Thoughts
Concerning Education

There were several editions of Some Thoughts Concerning Education; *Locke expanded and renumbered some of his paragraphs. The text given here is from the last edition, as printed in* The Works of John Locke, *(10 vols.; London, 1823), IX, 1–205. I have made a number of cuts, all of them minor; the entire substance and practically all the detail of Locke's argument have been preserved. For a slightly different selection, see John William Adamson,* The Educational Writings of John Locke *(2nd ed.; Cambridge, England, 1922), which has a fine introduction and useful notes; I am indebted to both.*

§ 1.   A sound mind in a sound body, is a short but full description of a happy state in this world: he that has these two, has little more to wish for; and he that wants either of them, will be but little the better for any thing else. Men's happiness or misery is most part of their own making. He whose mind directs not wisely, will never take the right way; and he whose body is crazy and feeble, will never be able to advance in it. I confess, there are some men's constitutions of body and mind so vigorous, and well framed by nature, that they need not much assistance from others; but, by the strength of their natural genius, they are, from their cradles, carried towards what is excellent; and, by the privilege of their happy constitu-

tions, are able to do wonders. But examples of this kind
are but few; and I think I may say, that, of all the men
we meet with, nine parts of ten are what they are, good
or evil, useful or not, by their education. It is that which
makes the great difference in mankind. The little, or almost insensible, impressions on our tender infancies, have
very important and lasting consequences: and there it is, as
in the fountains of some rivers, where a gentle application
of the hand turns the flexible waters into channels, that
make them take quite contrary courses; and by this little
direction, given them at first, in the source, they receive
different tendencies, and arrive at last at very remote and
distant places.

§ 2. I imagine the minds of children as easily turned,
this or that way, as water itself; and though this be the
principal part, and our main care should be about the
inside, yet the clay cottage is not to be neglected. I shall
therefore begin with the case, and consider first the health
of the body, as that which perhaps you may rather expect,
from that study I have been thought more peculiarly to
have applied myself to; and that also which will be
soonest despatched, as lying, if I guess not amiss, in a very
little compass.

§ 3. How necessary health is to our business and
happiness, and how requisite a strong constitution, able
to endure hardships and fatigue, is to one that will make
any figure in the world, is too obvious to need any proof.

§ 4. The consideration I shall here have, of health,
shall be, not what a physician ought to do, with a sick
or crazy child; but what the parents, without the help
of physic, should do for the preservation and improvement of an healthy, or, at least, not sickly constitution, in
their children: and this perhaps might be all despatched
in this one short rule, viz. that gentlemen should use their

children as the honest farmers and substantial yeomen do theirs. But because the mothers, possibly, may think this a little too hard, and the fathers, too short, I shall explain myself more particularly; only laying down this, as a general and certain observation for the women to consider, viz. that most children's constitutions are either spoiled, or at least harmed, by cockering and tenderness.

§ 9. Another thing, that is of great advantage to every one's health, but especially children's, is to be much in the open air, and very little, as may be, by the fire, even in winter. By this he will accustom himself also to heat and cold, shine and rain; all which if a man's body will not endure, it will serve him to very little purpose in this world: and when he is grown up, it is too late to begin to use him to it: it must be got early and by degrees. Thus the body may be brought to bear almost any thing. If I should advise him to play in the wind and sun without a hat, I doubt whether it could be borne. There would a thousand objections be made against it, which at last would amount to no more, in truth, than being sunburnt. And if my young master be to be kept always in the shade, and never exposed to the sun and wind, for fear of his complexion, it may be a good way to make him a beau, but not a man of business. And although greater regard be to be had to beauty in the daughters, yet I will take the liberty to say, that the more they are in the air, without prejudice to their faces, the stronger and healthier they will be; and the nearer they come to the hardships of their brothers in their education, the greater advantage will they receive from it, all the remaining part of their lives.

§ 10. Playing in the open air has but one danger in it, that I know: and that is, that when he is hot with running up and down, he should sit or lie down on the

cold or moist earth. This, I grant, and drinking cold
drink, when they are hot with labour or exercise, brings
more people to the grave, or to the brink of it, by fevers,
and other diseases, than any thing I know. These mischiefs are easily enough prevented, whilst he is little, being then seldom out of sight. And if during his childhood
he be constantly and rigorously kept from sitting on the
ground, or drinking any cold liquor, whilst he is hot,
the custom of forbearing, grown into a habit, will help
much to preserve him, when he is no longer under his
maid's or tutor's eye. This is all I think can be done in
the case. For, as years increase, liberty must come with
them; and, in a great many things, he must be trusted to
his own conduct, since there cannot always be a guard
upon him; except what you put into his own mind, by
good principles and established habits, which is the best
and surest, and therefore most to be taken care of. For,
from repeated cautions and rules, ever so often inculcated,
you are not to expect any thing, either in this or any
other case, farther than practice has established them into
habit.

§ 11. One thing the mention of the girls brings into
my mind, which must not be forgot; and that is, that
your son's clothes be never made strait, especially about
the breast. Let nature have scope to fashion the body as
she thinks best. She works of herself a great deal better
and exacter than we can direct her. And if women were
themselves to frame the bodies of their children in their
wombs, as they often endeavour to mend their shapes
when they are out, we should as certainly have no perfect
children born, as we have few well-shaped, that are strait-
laced, or much tampered with. This consideration should
methinks keep busy people (I will not say ignorant nurses
and boddice-makers) from meddling in a matter they

understand not; and they should be afraid to put nature out of her way, in fashioning the parts, when they know not how the least and meanest is made. And yet I have seen so many instances of children receiving great harm from strait lacing, that I cannot but conclude, there are other creatures, as well as monkeys, who, little wiser than they, destroy their young ones by senseless fondness, and too much embracing.

§ 12. Narrow breasts, short and stinking breath, ill lungs, and crookedness, are the natural and almost constant effects of hard boddice, and clothes that pinch. That way of making slender waists, and fine shapes, serves but the more effectually to spoil them. Nor can there, indeed, but be disproportion in the parts, when the nourishment, prepared in the several offices of the body, cannot be distributed, as nature designs. And therefore, what wonder is it, if, it being laid where it can, or some part not so braced, it often makes a shoulder, or a hip, higher or bigger than its just proportion? It is generally known, that the women of China, (imagining I know not what kind of beauty in it) by bracing and binding them hard from their infancy, have very little feet. I saw lately a pair of China shoes, which I was told were for a grown woman; they were so exceedingly disproportioned to the feet of one of the same age amongst us, that they would scarce have been big enough for one of our little girls. Besides this, it is observed, that their women are also very little, and short-lived; whereas the men are of the ordinary stature of other men, and live to a proportionable age. These defects in the female sex of that country are by some imputed to the unreasonable binding of their feet; whereby the free circulation of the blood is hindered, and the growth and health of the whole body suffers. And how often do we see, that some small part of the foot being injured, by a wrench or a blow, the whole leg or thigh thereby loses its strength and nourishment, and dwindles away! How much greater inconveniences may we expect, when the thorax, wherein is placed the heart and seat of life, is unnaturally compressed, and hindered from its due expansion!

§ 13. As for his diet, it ought to be very plain and simple; and, if I might advise, flesh should be forborn as long as he is in coats, or at least, till he is two or three years old. But whatever advantage this may be, to his present and future health and strength, I fear it will hardly be consented to, by parents, misled by the custom of eating too much flesh themselves; who will be apt to think their children, as they do themselves, in danger to be starved, if they have not flesh, at least twice a day. This I am sure, children would breed their teeth with much less danger, be freer from diseases, whilst they were little, and lay the foundations of an healthy and strong constitution much surer, if they were not crammed so much as they are, by fond mothers and foolish servants, and were kept wholly from flesh, the first three or four years of their lives.

But if my young master must needs have flesh, let it be but once a day, and of one sort, at a meal. Plain beef, mutton, veal, &c. without other sauce than hunger, is best: and great care should be used, that he eat bread plentifully both alone and with every thing else. And whatever he eats, that is solid, make him chew it well. We English are often negligent herein; from whence follows indigestion, and other great inconveniencies.

§ 15. As to his meals, I should think it best, that, as much as it can be conveniently avoided, they should not be kept constantly to an hour. For, when custom hath fixed his eating to certain stated periods, his stomach will expect victuals at the usual hour, and grow peevish if he passes it; either fretting itself into a troublesome excess, or flagging into a downright want of appetite. Therefore I would have no time kept constantly to for his breakfast, dinner, and supper, but rather varied, almost every day. And if, betwixt these, which I call meals, he will eat, let him have, as often as he calls for it, good dry bread. If any one think this too hard and sparing a diet for a child, let them know, that a child will never starve, nor dwindle for want of nourishment, who, besides flesh at dinner, and spoon-meat, or some such other thing at supper, may have good bread and beer, as often as he has a stomach: for thus, upon second thoughts, I should judge it best for children to be ordered. The morning is generally designed for study, to which a full stomach is but an ill preparation. Dry bread, though the best nourishment, has the least temptation: and nobody would have a child crammed at breakfast, who has any regard to his mind or body, and would not have him dull and unhealthy. Nor let any one think this unsuitable to one of estate and condition. A gentleman, in any age, ought to be so bred, as to be fitted to bear arms, and be a soldier. But he that in this, breeds his son so, as if he designed him to sleep over his life, in the plenty and ease of a full fortune he intends to leave him, little considers the examples he has seen, or the age he lives in.

§ 16. His drink should be only small beer; and that too he should never be suffered to have between meals, but after he had eat a piece of bread.

§ 30. And thus I have done with what concerns the body and health, which reduces itself to these few and easily observable rules. Plenty of open air, exercise, and sleep; plain diet, no wine or strong drink, and very little or no physic; not too warm and strait clothing; especially the head and feet kept cold, and the feet often used to cold water and exposed to wet.

§ 31. Due care being had to keep the body in strength and vigour, so that it may be able to obey and execute the orders of the mind; the next and principal business is, to set the mind right, that on all occasions it may be disposed to consent to nothing but what may be suitable to the dignity and excellency of a rational creature.

§ 32. If what I have said in the beginning of this discourse be true, as I do not doubt but it is, viz. that the difference to be found in the manners and abilities of men is owing more to their education than to any thing else; we have reason to conclude, that great care is to be had of the forming children's minds, and giving them that seasoning early, which shall influence their lives always after. For when they do well or ill, the praise or blame will be laid there: and when any thing is done awkwardly, the common saying will pass upon them, that it is suitable to their breeding.

§ 33. As the strength of the body lies chiefly in being able to endure hardships, so also does that of the mind. And the great principle and foundation of all virtue and worth is placed in this, that a man is able to deny himself his own desires, cross his own inclinations, and purely follow what reason directs as best, though the appetite lean the other way.

§ 34. The great mistake I have observed in people's breeding their children has been, that this has not been taken care enough of in its due season; that the mind has not been made obedient to discipline, and pliant to reason, when at first it was most tender, most easy to be bowed. Parents being wisely ordained by nature to love their children, are very apt, if reason watch not that natural affection very warily; are apt, I say, to let it run into fondness. They love their little ones, and it is their duty: but they often with them cherish their faults too. They must not be crossed, forsooth; they must be permitted to have their wills in all things; and they being in their infancies not capable of great vices, their parents think they may safely enough indulge their little irregularities, and make themselves sport with that pretty perverseness, which they think well enough becomes that innocent age. But to a fond parent, that would not have his child corrected for a perverse trick, but excused it, saying it was a small matter; Solon very well replied, "Ay, but custom is a great one."

§ 35. The fondling must be taught to strike, and call names; must have what he cries for, and do what he pleases. Thus parents, by humouring and cockering them when little, corrupt the principles of nature in their children, and wonder afterwards to taste the bitter waters, when they themselves have poisoned the fountain. For when their children are grown up, and these ill habits with them; when they are now too big to be dandled, and their parents can no longer make use of them as playthings; then they complain that the brats are untoward and perverse; then they are offended to see them wilful, and are troubled with those ill humours, which they themselves infused and fomented in them; and then, perhaps too late, would be glad to get out those weeds which their own hands have planted, and which now have taken too deep root to be easily extirpated. For he that has been used to have his will in every thing, as long as he was in coats, why should we think it strange that he should desire it and contend for it still, when he is in breeches? Indeed, as he grows more towards a man, age shows his faults the more, so that there be few parents then so blind, as not to see them; few so insensible as not to feel the ill effects of their own indulgence. He had the will of his maid before he could speak or go; he had the mastery of his parents ever since he could prattle; and why, now he is grown up, is stronger and wiser than he was then, why now of a sudden must he be restrained and curbed? why must he at seven, fourteen, or twenty years old, lose the privilege which the parent's indulgence, till then, so largely allowed him? Try it in a dog, or a horse, or any other creature, and see whether the ill and resty tricks they have learned when young are easily to be mended when they are knit: and yet none of those creatures are half so wilful and proud, or half so desirous to be masters of themselves and others, as man.

§ 38. It seems plain to me, that the principle of all virtue and excellency lies in a power of denying ourselves the satisfaction of our own desires, where reason does not authorize them. This power is to be got and improved by custom, made easy and familiar by an early practice. If therefore I might be heard, I would advise, that, contrary to the ordinary way, children should be used to submit their desires, and go without their longings, even from their very cradles. The very first thing they should learn to know, should be, that they were not to have any thing, because it pleased them, but because it was thought fit for them. If things suitable to their wants were supplied to them, so that they were never suffered to have what they once cried for, they would learn to be content without it; would never with bawling and peevishness contend for mastery; nor be half so uneasy to themselves and others as they are, because from the first beginning they are not thus handled. If they were never suffered to obtain their desire by the impatience they expressed for it, they would no more cry for other things than they do for the moon.

§ 39. I say not this as if children were not to be indulged in any thing, or that I expected they should, in hanging-sleeves, have the reason and conduct of counsellors. I consider them as children, who must be tenderly used, who must play, and have play things. That which I mean is, that whenever they craved what was not fit for them to have, or do, they should not be permitted it, because they were little and desired it: nay, whatever they were importunate for, they should be sure, for that very reason, to be denied.

§ 40. Those therefore that intend ever to govern their children, should begin it whilst they are very little; and look that they perfectly comply with the will of their parents. Would you have your son obedient to you, when past a child? Be sure then to establish the authority of a father, as soon as he is capable of submission, and can understand in whose power he is. If you would have him stand in awe of you, imprint it in his infancy; and, as he approaches more to a man, admit him nearer to your familiarity: so shall you have him your obedient subject (as is fit) whilst he is a child, and your affectionate friend when he is a man. For methinks they mightily misplace the treatment due to their children, who are indulgent and familiar when they are little, but severe to them, and keep them at a distance, when they are grown up. For liberty and indulgence can do no good to children: their want of judgment makes them stand in need of restraint and discipline. And, on the contrary, imperiousness and severity is but an ill way of treating men, who have reason of their own to guide them, unless you have a mind to make your children, when grown up, weary of you; and secretly to say within themselves, "When will you die, father?"

§ 41. I imagine every one will judge it reasonable,

that their children, when little, should look upon their parents as their lords, their absolute governors; and, as such, stand in awe of them: and that, when they come to riper years, they should look on them as their best, as their only sure friends: and, as such, love and reverence them. The way I have mentioned, if I mistake not, is the only one to obtain this. We must look upon our children, when grown up, to be like ourselves; with the same passions, the same desires. We would be thought rational creatures, and have our freedom; we love not to be uneasy under constant rebukes and brow-beatings; nor can we bear severe humours, and great distance, in those we converse with. Whoever has such treatment when he is a man, will look out other company, other friends, other conversation, with whom he can be at ease. If therefore a strict hand be kept over children from the beginning, they will in that age be tractable, and quietly submit to it, as never having known any other: and if, as they grow up to the use of reason, the rigour of government be, as they deserve it, gently relaxed, the father's brow more smoothed to them, and the distance by degrees abated: his former restraints will increase their love, when they find it was only a kindness for them, and a care to make them capable to deserve the favour of their parents, and the esteem of every body else.

§ 42. Thus much for the settling your authority over children in general. Fear and awe ought to give you the first power over their minds, and love and friendship in riper years to hold it: for the time must come, when they will be past the rod and correction; and then, if the love of you make them not obedient and dutiful; if the love of virtue and reputation keep them not in laudable courses; I ask, what hold will you have upon them, to turn them to it? Indeed, fear of having a scanty portion, if they displease you, may make them slaves to your estate; but they will be nevertheless ill and wicked in private, and that restraint will not last always. Every man must some time or other be trusted to himself, and his own conduct; and he that is a good, a virtuous, and able man, must be made so within. And therefore, what he is to receive from education, what is to sway and influence his life, must be something put into him betimes: habits woven into the very principles of his nature; and not a counterfeit carriage, and dissembled outside, put on by fear, only to avoid the present anger of a father, who perhaps may disinherit him.

§ 43. This being laid down in general, as the course ought to be taken, it is fit we come now to consider the parts of the discipline to be used, a little more particularly. I have spoken so much of carrying a strict hand over children, that perhaps I shall be suspected of not considering enough what is due to their tender age and constitutions. But that opinion will vanish, when you have heard me a little farther. For I am very apt to think, that great severity of punishment does but very little good; nay, great harm in education: and I believe it will be found, that, cæteris paribus, those children who have been most chastised, seldom make the best men. All that I have hitherto contended for, is, that whatsoever rigour is necessary, it is more to be used, the younger children are; and, having by a due application wrought its effect, it is to be relaxed, and changed into a milder sort of government.

§ 44. A compliance, and suppleness of their wills, being by a steady hand introduced by parents, before children have memories to retain the beginnings of it, will seem natural to them, and work afterwards in them, as if it were so; preventing all occasions of struggling, or

repining. The only care is, that it be begun early, and in-
flexibly kept to, till awe and respect be grown familiar,
and there appears not the least reluctancy in the submission and ready obedience of their minds. When this
reverence is once thus established, (which it must be
early, or else it will cost pains and blows to recover it,
and the more, the longer it is deferred) it is by it, mixed
still with as much indulgence as they made not an ill use
of, and not by beating, chiding, or other servile punishments, they are for the future to be governed, as they
grow up to more understanding.

§ 45. That this is so, will be easily allowed, when it
is but considered what is to be aimed at, in an ingenuous
education; and upon what it turns.

1. He that has not a mastery over his inclinations, he
that knows not how to resist the importunity of present
pleasure or pain, for the sake of what reason tells him is
fit to be done, wants the true principle of virtue and industry; and is in danger of never being good for any thing.
This temper, therefore, so contrary to unguided nature,
is to be got betimes; and this habit, as the true foundation of future ability and happiness, is to be wrought into
the mind, as early as may be, even from the first dawn-
ings of any knowledge or apprehension in children; and
so to be confirmed in them, by all the care and ways
imaginable, by those who have the oversight of their
education.

§ 46. 2. On the other side, if the mind be curbed, and
humbled too much in children; if their spirits be abased
and broken much, by too strict an hand over them; they
lose all their vigour and industry, and are in a worse state
than the former. For extravagant young fellows, that have
liveliness and spirit, come sometimes to be set right, and
so make able and great men: but dejected minds, tim-

orous and tame, and low spirits, are hardly ever to be raised, and very seldom attain to any thing. To avoid the danger that is on either hand is the great art: and he that has found a way how to keep up a child's spirit, easy, active, and free; and yet, at the same time, to restrain him from many things he has a mind to, and to draw him to things that are uneasy to him; he, I say, that knows how to reconcile these seeming contradictions, has, in my opinion, got the true secret of education.

§ 47. The usual lazy and short way by chastisement, and the rod, which is the only instrument of government that tutors generally know, or ever think of, is the most unfit of any to be used in education; because it tends to both those mischiefs; which, as we have shown, are the Scylla and Charybdis, which, on the one hand or the other, ruin all that miscarry.

§ 48. 1. This kind of punishment contributes not at all to the mastery of our natural propensity to indulge corporal and present pleasure, and to avoid pain at any rate; but rather encourages it; and thereby strengthens that in us, which is the root, from whence spring all vicious actions and the irregularities of life. From what other motive, but of sensual pleasure, and pain, does a child act, who drudges at his book against his inclination, or abstains from eating unwholesome fruit, that he takes pleasure in, only out of fear of whipping? He in this only prefers the greater corporal pleasure, or avoids the greater corporal pain. And what is it to govern his actions, and direct his conduct, by such motives as these? what is it, I say, but to cherish that principle in him, which it is our business to root out and destroy? And therefore I cannot think any correction useful to a child, where the shame of suffering for having done amiss does not work more upon him than the pain.

§ 49. 2. This sort of correction naturally breeds an aversion to that which it is the tutor's business to create a liking to. How obvious is it to observe, that children come to hate things which were at first acceptable to them, when they find themselves whipped, and chid, and teazed about them? And it is not to be wondered at in them; when grown men would not be able to be reconciled to any thing by such ways. Who is there that would not be disgusted with any innocent recreation, in itself indifferent to him, if he should with blows, or ill language, be hauled to it, when he had no mind? or be constantly so treated, for some circumstances in his application to it? This is natural to be so. Offensive circumstances ordinarily infect innocent things, which they are joined with: and the very sight of a cup, wherein any one uses to take nauseous physic, turns his stomach; so that nothing will relish well out of it, though the cup be ever so clean, and well-shaped, and of the richest materials.

§ 50. 3. Such a sort of slavish discipline makes a slavish temper. The child submits, and dissembles obedience, whilst the fear of the rod hangs over him; but when that is removed, and, by being out of sight, he can promise himself impunity, he gives the greater scope to his natural inclination; which by this way is not at all altered, but on the contrary heightened and increased in him; and after such restraint, breaks out usually with the more violence. Or,

§ 51. 4. If severity carried to the highest pitch does prevail, and works a cure upon the present unruly distemper, it is often bringing in the room of it worse and more dangerous disease, by breaking the mind; and then, in the place of a disorderly young fellow, you have a low-spirited moped creature: who, however with his unnatural sobriety he may please silly people, who commend tame inactive children, because they make no noise, nor give them any trouble; yet, at last, will probably prove as uncomfortable a thing to his friends, as he will be, all his life, an useless thing to himself and others.

§ 52. Beating then, and all other sorts of slavish and corporal punishments, are not the discipline fit to be used in the education of those who would have wise, good, and ingenuous men; and therefore very rarely to be applied, and that only on great occasions, and cases of extremity. On the other side, to flatter children by rewards of things that are pleasant to them, is as carefully to be avoided. He that will give to his son apples, or sugar-plums, or what else of this kind he is most delighted with, to make him learn his book, does but authorise his love of pleasure, and cocker up that dangerous propensity, which he ought by all means to subdue and stifle in him. You can never hope to teach him to master it, whilst you compound for the check you give his inclination in one place, by the satisfaction you propose to it in another. To make a good, a wise, and a virtuous man, it is fit he should learn to cross his appetite, and deny his inclination to riches, finery, or pleasing his palate, &c. whenever his reason advises the contrary, and his duty requires it. But when you draw him to do any thing that is fit, by the offer of money; or reward the pains of learning his book, by the pleasure of a luscious morsel; when you promise him a lace-cravat, or a fine new suit, upon performance of some of his little tasks; what do you, by proposing these as rewards, but allow them to be the good things he should aim at, and thereby encourage his longing for them, and accustom him to place his happiness in them? Thus people, to prevail with children to be industrious about their grammar, dancing, or some other such matter, of no great moment to the happiness or usefulness of their lives, by misapplied rewards and punishments, sacrifice their virtue, invert the order of their education, and teach them luxury, pride, or covetousness, &c. For in this way, flattering those wrong inclinations, which they should restrain and suppress, they lay the foundations of those future vices, which cannot be avoided, but by curbing our desires, and accustoming them early to submit to reason.

§ 54. But if you take away the rod on one hand, and these little encouragements, which they are taken with, on the other; how then (will you say) shall children be governed? Remove hope and fear, and there is an end of all discipline. I grant, that good and evil, reward and punishment, are the only motives to a rational creature; these are the spur and reins, whereby all mankind are set on work and guided, and therefore they are to be made use of to children too. For I advise their parents and governors always to carry this in their minds, that children are to be treated as rational creatures.

§ 56. The rewards and punishments then whereby we should keep children in order are quite of another kind; and of that force, that when we can get them once to work, the business, I think, is done, and the difficulty is over. Esteem and disgrace are, of all others, the most powerful incentives to the mind, when once it is brought to relish them. If you can once get into children a love of credit, and an apprehension of shame and disgrace, you have put into them the true principle, which will constantly work, and incline them to the right. But it will be asked, How shall this be done?

I confess, it does not, at first appearance, want some difficulty; but yet I think it worth our while to seek the ways (and practise them when found) to attain this, which I look on as the great secret of education.

§ 57. First, children (earlier perhaps than we think) are very sensible of praise and commendation. They find a pleasure in being esteemed and valued, especially by their parents, and those whom they depend on. If therefore the father caress and commend them, when they do well; show a cold and neglectful countenance to them upon doing ill; and this accompanied by a like carriage of the mother, and all others that are about them; it will in a little time make them sensible of the difference: and this, if constantly observed, I doubt not but will of itself work more than threats or blows, which lose their force, when once grown common, and are of no use when shame does not attend them; and therefore are to be forborn, and never to be used, but in the case hereafter mentioned, when it is brought to extremity.

§ 58. But, secondly, to make the sense of esteem or disgrace sink the deeper, and be of the more weight, other agreeable or disagreeable things should constantly accompany these different states; not as particular rewards and punishments of this or that particular action, but as necessarily belonging to, and constantly attending one, who by his carriage has brought himself into a state of disgrace or commendation. By which way of treating them, children may as much as possible be brought to conceive, that those that are commended and in esteem for doing well, will necessarily be beloved and cherished by every body, and have all other good things as a consequence of it; and, on the other side, when any one by miscarriage falls into dis-esteem, and cares not to preserve his credit, he will unavoidably fall under neglect and contempt: and, in that state, the want of whatever might satisfy or delight him, will follow. In this way the objects of their desires are made assisting to virtue; when a settled experience from the beginning teaches children,

that the things they delight in, belong to, and are to be
enjoyed by those only, who are in a state of reputation.
If by these means you can come once to shame them out
of their faults, (for besides that, I would willingly have
no punishment) and make them in love with the pleasure
of being well thought on, you may turn them as you
please, and they will be in love with all the ways of virtue.

§ 59. The great difficulty here is, I imagine, from the
folly and perverseness of servants, who are hardly to be
hindered from crossing herein the design of the father
and mother. Children, discountenanced by their parents
for any fault, find usually a refuge and relief in the ca-
resses of those foolish flatterers, who thereby undo whatever the parents endeavour to establish. When the father
or mother looks sour on the child, every body else should
put on the same coldness to him, and nobody give him
countenance, till forgiveness asked, and a reformation of
his fault, has set him right again, and restored him to his
former credit. If this were constantly observed, I guess
there would be little need of blows or chiding: their own
ease and satisfaction would quickly teach children to
court commendation, and avoid doing that, which they
found every body condemned, and they were sure to
suffer for, without being chid or beaten. This would
teach them modesty and shame; and they would quickly
come to have a natural abhorrence for that, which they
found made them slighted and neglected by every body.
But how this inconvenience from servants is to be reme-
died, I must leave to parents' care and consideration. Only
I think it of great importance; and that they are very
happy, who can get discreet people about their children.

§ 60. Frequent beating or chiding is therefore carefully to be avoided; because this sort of correction never
produces any good, farther than it serves to raise shame

and abhorrence of the miscarriage that brought it on them. And if the greatest part of the trouble be not the sense that they have done amiss, and the apprehension that they have drawn on themselves the just displeasure of their best friends, the pain of whipping will work but an imperfect cure. It only patches up for the present, and skins it over, but reaches not to the bottom of the sore. Ingenuous shame, and the apprehension of displeasure, are the only true restraints: these alone ought to hold the reins, and keep the child in order. But corporal punishments must necessarily lose that effect, and wear out the sense of shame, where they frequently return. Shame in children has the same place that modesty has in women; which cannot be kept, and often transgressed against. And as to the apprehension of displeasure in the parents, they will come to be very insignificant, if the marks of that displeasure quickly cease, and a few blows fully expiate. Parents should well consider, what faults in their children are weighty enough to deserve the declaration of their anger: but when their displeasure is once declared to a degree that carries any punishment with it, they ought not presently to lay by the severity of their brows, but to restore their children to their former grace with some difficulty; and delay a full reconciliation, till their conformity, and more than ordinary merit, make good their amendment. If this be not so ordered, punishment will, by familiarity, become a mere thing of course, and lose all its influence: offending, being chastised, and then forgiven, will be thought as natural and necessary as noon, night, and morning, following one another.

§ 63. But if a right course be taken with children, there will not be so much need of the application of the common rewards and punishments, as we imagined, and as the general practice has established. For all their innocent folly, playing, and childish actions, are to be left perfectly free and unrestrained, as far as they can consist with the respect due to those that are present; and that with the greatest allowance. If these faults of their age, rather than of the children themselves, were, as they should be, left only to time, and imitation, and riper years to cure, children would escape a great deal of mis-applied and useless correction; which either fails to over-power the natural disposition of their childhood, and so, by an ineffectual familiarity, makes correction in other necessary cases of less use; or else if it be of force to re-strain the natural gaiety of that age, it serves only to spoil the temper both of body and mind. If the noise and bustle of their play prove at any time inconvenient, or unsuitable to the place or company they are in, (which can only be where their parents are) a look or a word from the father or mother, if they have established the authority they should, will be enough either to remove, or quiet them for that time. But this gamesome humour, which is wisely adapted by nature to their age and temper, should rather be encouraged, to keep up their spirits, and improve their strength and health, than curbed or restrained: and the chief art is to make all that they have to do, sport and play too.

§ 64. And here give me leave to take notice of one thing I think a fault in the ordinary method of educa-tion; and that is, the charging of children's memories, upon all occasions, with rules and precepts, which they often do not understand, and are constantly as soon for-got as given. If it be some action you would have done, or done otherwise; whenever they forget, or do it awk-wardly, make them do it over and over again, till they are perfect: whereby you will get these two advantages: first, to see whether it be an action they can do, or is fit to be expected of them. For sometimes children are bid to do things, which, upon trial, they are found not able to do; and had need be taught and exercised in, before they are required to do them. But it is much easier for a tutor to command, than to teach. Secondly, another thing got by it will be this, that by repeating the same action, till it be grown habitual in them, the performance will not depend on memory, or reflection, the concomitant of prudence and age, and not of childhood; but will be natural in them. Thus, bowing to a gentleman when he salutes him, and looking in his face when he speaks to him, is by constant use as natural to a well-bred man, as breathing; it requires no thought, no reflection. Having this way cured in your child any fault, it is cured for ever: and thus, one by one, you may weed them out all, and plant what habits you please.

§ 65. I have seen parents so heap rules on their children, that it was impossible for the poor little ones to remember a tenth part of them, much less to observe them. However, they were either by words or blows corrected for the breach of those multipled and often very impertinent precepts. Whence it naturally followed, that the children minded not what was said to them; when it was evident to them, that no attention they were capable of, was sufficient to preserve them from transgression, and the rebukes which followed it.

Let therefore your rules to your son be as few as is possible, and rather fewer than more than seem absolutely necessary. For if you burden him with many rules, one of these two things must necessarily follow, that either he must be very often punished, which will be of ill consequence, by making punishment too frequent and familiar; or else you must let the transgressions of some of your rules go unpunished, whereby they will of course grow contemptible, and your authority become cheap to him. Make but few laws, but see they be well observed, when once made. Few years require but few laws; and as his age increases, when one rule is by practice well established, you may add another.

§ 66. But pray remember, children are not to be taught by rules, which will be always slipping out of their memories. What you think necessary for them to do, settle in them by an indispensable practice, as often as the occasion returns; and, if it be possible, make occasions. This will beget habits in them, which, being once established, operate of themselves easily and naturally, without the assistance of the memory. But here let me give two cautions: 1. The one is, that you keep them to the practice of what you would have grow into a habit in them, by kind words and gentle admonitions, rather as minding them of what they forget, than by harsh rebukes and chiding, as if they were wilfully guilty. 2dly, Another thing you are to take care of, is, not to endeavour to settle too many habits at once, lest by a variety you confound them, and so perfect none. When constant custom has made any one thing easy and natural to them, and they practise it without reflection, you may then go on to another.

This method of teaching children by a repeated practice, and the same action done over and over again, under the eye and direction of the tutor, till they have got the habit of doing it well, and not by relying on rules trusted to their memories; has so many advantages, which way soever we consider it, that I cannot but wonder (if ill customs could be wondered at in any thing) how it could possibly be so much neglected. I shall name one more that comes now in my way. By this method we shall see, whether what is required of him be adapted to his capacity, and any way suited to the child's natural genius and constitution: for that too must be considered in a right education. We must not hope wholly to change their original tempers, nor make the gay pensive and grave, nor the melancholy sportive, without spoiling them. God has stamped certain characters upon men's minds, which, like their shapes, may perhaps be a little mended; but can hardly be totally altered and transformed into the contrary.

He therefore, that is about children, should well study their natures and aptitudes, and see, by often trials, what turn they easily take, and what becomes them; observe what their native stock is, how it may be improved, and what it is fit for: he should consider what they want, whether they be capable of having it wrought into them by industry, and incorporated there by practice; and whether it be worth while to endeavour it. For, in many cases, all that we can do, or should aim at, is, to make the best of what nature has given, to prevent the vices and faults to which such a constitution is most inclined, and give it all the advantages it is capable of. Every one's natural genius should be carried as far as it could; but to attempt the putting another upon him, will be but labour in vain; and what is so plaistered on will at best sit but untowardly, and have always hanging to it the ungracefulness of constraint and affectation.

Affectation is not, I confess, an early fault of childhood, or the product of untaught nature: it is of that sort of weeds, which grow not in the wild uncultivated waste, but in garden-plots, under the negligent hand, or unskilful care of a gardener. Management and instruction, and some sense of the necessity of breeding, are requisite to make any one capable of affectation, which endeavours to correct natural defects, and has always the laudable aim of pleasing, though it always misses it; and the more it labours to put on gracefulness, the farther it is from it. For this reason it is the more carefully to be watched, because it is the proper fault of education; a perverted education indeed, but such as young people often fall into, either by their own mistake, or the ill conduct of those about them.

He that will examine wherein that gracefulness lies, which always pleases, will find it arises from that natural coherence, which appears between the thing done, and such a temper of mind, as cannot but be approved of as suitable to the occasion. We cannot but be pleased with an humane, friendly, civil temper, wherever we meet with it. A mind free, and master of itself and all its actions, not low and narrow, not haughty and insolent, not blemished with any great defect; is what every one is taken with. The actions, which naturally flow from such a well-formed mind, please us also, as the genuine marks of it; and being, as it were, natural emanations from the spirit and disposition within, cannot but be easy and unconstrained. This seems to me to be that beauty, which shines through some men's actions, sets off all that they do, and takes with all they come near; when by a constant practice they have fashioned their carriage, and made all those little expressions of civility and respect, which nature or custom has established in conversation, so easy to themselves, that they seem not artificial or studied, but naturally to follow from a sweetness of mind and a well-turned disposition.

On the other side, affectation is an awkward and forced imitation of what should be genuine and easy, wanting the beauty that accompanies what is natural; because there is always a disagreement between the outward action, and the mind within, one of these two ways:

1. Either when a man would outwardly put on a disposition of mind, which then he really has not, but endeavours by a forced carriage to make show of; yet so, that the constraint he is under discovers itself: and thus men affect sometimes to appear sad, merry, or kind, when, in truth, they are not so.

2. The other is, when they do not endeavour to make show of dispositions of mind which they have not, but to express those they have by a carriage not suited to them: and such in conversation are all constrained motions, actions, words, or looks, which, though designed to show either their respect or civility to the company, or their satisfaction and easiness in it, are not yet natural nor genuine marks of the one or the other; but rather of some defect or mistake within. Imitation of others, without discerning what is graceful in them, or what is peculiar to their characters, often makes a great part of this. But affectation of all kinds, whencesoever it proceeds, is always offensive: because we naturally hate whatever is counterfeit; and condemn those who have nothing better to recommend themselves by.

Plain and rough nature, left to itself, is much better than an artificial ungracefulness, and such studied ways of being ill-fashioned. The want of an accomplishment, or some defect in our behaviour, coming short of the utmost gracefulness, often escapes observation and censure. But affectation in any part of our carriage is lighting up a candle to our defects; and never fails to make us be taken notice of, either as wanting sense, or wanting sincerity. This governors ought the more diligently to look after, because, as I above observed, it is an acquired ugliness, owing to mistaken education; few being guilty of it, but those who pretend to breeding, and would not be thought ignorant of what is fashionable and becoming in conversation: and, if I mistake not, it has often its rise from the lazy admonitions of those who give rules, and propose examples, without joining practice with their instructions, and making their pupils repeat the action in their sight, that they may correct what is indecent or constrained in it, till it be perfected into an habitual and becoming easiness.

§ 67. Manners, as they call it, about which children are so often perplexed, and have so many goodly exhortations made them, by their wise maids and governesses, I think, are rather to be learned by example than rules; and then children, if kept out of ill company, will take a pride to behave themselves prettily, after the fashion of others, perceiving themselves esteemed and commended for it. But if, by a little negligence in this part, the boy should not put off his hat, nor make legs very gracefully, a dancing-master will cure that defect, and wipe off all that plainness of nature, which the à-la-mode people call clownishness. And since nothing appears to me to give children so much becoming confidence and behaviour, and so to raise them to the conversation of those above their age, as dancing; I think they should be taught to dance, as soon as they are capable of learning it. For, though this consist only in outward gracefulness of motion, yet, I know not how, it gives children manly thoughts and carriage, more than any thing. But otherwise I would not have little children much tormented about punctilios, or niceties of breeding.

Never trouble yourself about those faults in them which you know age will cure.

§ 68. I mentioned above, one great mischief that came by servants to children, when by their flatteries they take off the edge and force of the parents' rebukes, and so lessen their authority. And here is another great inconvenience, which children receive from the ill examples which they meet with amongst the meaner servants.

They are wholly, if possible, to be kept from such conversation: for the contagion of these ill precedents, both in civility and virtue, horribly infects children, as often as they come within reach of it. They frequently learn, from unbred or debauched servants, such language, untowardly tricks and vices, as otherwise they possibly would be ignorant of all their lives.

§ 69. It is a hard matter wholly to prevent this mischief. You will have very good luck, if you never have a clownish or vicious servant, and if from them your children never get any infection. But yet, as much must be done towards it as can be; and the children kept as much as may be in the company of their parents, and those to whose care they are committed. To this purpose, their being in their presence should be made easy to them: they should be allowed the liberties and freedom suitable to their ages, and not be held under unnecessary restraints, when in their parent's or governor's sight. If it be a prison to them, it is no wonder they should not like it. They must not be hindered from being children, or from playing, or doing as children; but from doing ill. All other liberty is to be allowed them. Next, to make them in love with the company of their parents, they should receive all their good things there, and from their hands. The servants should be hindered from making court to them, by giving them strong drink, wine, fruit, playthings, and other such matters, which may make them in love with their conversation.

§ 70. Having named company, I am almost ready to throw away my pen, and trouble you no farther on this subject. For since that does more than all precepts, rules, and instructions, methinks it is almost wholly in vain to make a long discourse of other things, and to talk of that almost to no purpose. For you will be ready to say, "What shall I do with my son? If I keep him always at home, he will be in danger to be my young master; and if I send him abroad, how is it possible to keep him from the contagion of rudeness and vice, which is every where so in fashion? In my house he will perhaps be more innocent, but more ignorant too of the world: wanting there change of company, and being used constantly to the same faces, he will, when he comes abroad, be a sheepish or conceited creature."

I confess, both sides have their inconveniencies. Being abroad, it is true, will make him bolder, and better able to bustle and shift amongst boys of his own age; and the emulation of schoolfellows often puts life and industry into young lads. But till you can find a school, wherein it is possible for the master to look after the manners of his scholars, and can show as great effects of his care of forming their minds to virtue, and their carriage to good breeding, as of forming their tongues to the learned languages; you must confess, that you have a strange value for words, when, preferring the languages of the ancient Greeks and Romans to that which made them such brave men, you think it worth while to hazard your son's innocence and virtue for a little Greek and Latin. For, as for that boldness and spirit which lads get amongst their playfellows at school, it has ordinarily such a mixture of rudeness and an ill-turned confidence, that those misbecoming and disingenuous ways of shifting in the world must be unlearned, and all the tincture washed out again, to make way for better principles, and such manners as make a truly worthy man. He that considers how diametrically opposite the skill of living well, and managing, as a man should do, his affairs in the world, is to that malapertness, tricking, or violence, learnt among schoolboys, will think the faults of a privater education infinitely to be preferred to such improvements; and will take care to preserve his child's innocence and modesty at home, as being nearer of kin, and more in the way of those qualities, which make an useful and able man. Nor does any one find, or so much as suspect, that that retirement and bashfulness, which their daughters are brought up in, makes them less knowing or less able women. Conversation, when they come into the world, soon gives them a becoming assurance; and whatsoever, beyond that, there is of rough and boisterous, may in men be very well spared too: for courage and steadiness, as I take it, lie not in roughness and ill breeding.

Virtue is harder to be got than a knowledge of the world; and, if lost in a young man, is seldom recovered. Sheepishness and ignorance of the world, the faults imputed to a private education, are neither the necessary consequences of being bred at home; nor, if they were, are they incurable evils. Vice is the more stubborn, as well as the more dangerous evil of the two; and therefore, in the first place, to be fenced against. If that sheepish softness, which often enervates those who are bred like fondlings at home, be carefully to be avoided, it is principally so for virtue's sake; for fear lest such a yielding temper should be too susceptible of vicious impressions, and expose the novice too easily to be corrupted. A young man, before he leaves the shelter of his father's house, and the guard of a tutor, should be fortified with resolution, and made acquainted with men, to secure his virtue; lest he should be led into some ruinous course, or fatal precipice, before he is sufficiently acquainted with the dangers of conversation, and has steadiness enough not to yield to every temptation. Were it not for this, a

young man's bashfulness and ignorance of the world
would not so much need an early care. Conversation
would cure it in a great measure; or, if that will not do it
early enough, it is only a stronger reason for a good tutor
at home. For, if pains be to be taken to give him a manly
air and assurance betimes, it is chiefly as a fence to his
virtue, when he goes into the world, under his own conduct.

It is preposterous, therefore, to sacrifice his innocency
to the attaining of confidence, and some little skill of
bustling for himself among others, by his conversation
with ill-bred and vicious boys; when the chief use of that
sturdiness, and standing upon his own legs, is only for the
preservation of his virtue. For if confidence or cunning
come once to mix with vice, and support his miscarriages,
he is only the surer lost; and you must undo again, and strip
him of that he has got from his companions, or give him
up to ruin. Boys will unavoidably be taught assurance by
conversation with men, when they are brought into it;
and that is time enough. Modesty and submission, till
then, better fits them for instruction: and therefore there
needs not any great care to stock them with confidence
beforehand. That which requires most time, pains, and
assiduity, is to work into them the principles and practice
of virtue and good breeding. This is the seasoning they
should be prepared with, so as not easily to be got out
again: this they had need to be well provided with. For
conversation, when they come into the world, will add to
their knowledge and assurance, but be too apt to take
from their virtue; which therefore they ought to be plentifully stored with, and have that tincture sunk deep into
them.

How they should be fitted for conversation, and entered into the world, when they are ripe for it, we shall

consider in another place. But how any one's being put into a mixed herd of unruly boys, and there learning to wrangle at trap, or rook at span-farthing, fits him for civil conversation or business, I do not see. And what qualities are ordinarily to be got from such a troop of playfellows as schools usually assemble together, from parents of all kinds, that a father should so much covet it, is hard to divine. I am sure, he who is able to be at the charge of a tutor at home, may there give his son a more genteel carriage, more manly thoughts, and a sense of what is worthy and becoming, with a greater proficiency in learning into the bargain, and ripen him up sooner into a man, than any at school can do. Not that I blame the schoolmaster in this, or think it to be laid to his charge. The difference is great between two or three pupils in the same house, and three or fourscore boys lodged up and down. For, let the master's industry and skill be ever so great, it is impossible he should have 50 or 100 scholars under his eye any longer than they are in the school together: nor can it be expected, that he should instruct them successfully in any thing but their books; the forming of their minds and manners requiring a constant attention and particular application to every single boy; which is impossible in a numerous flock, and would be wholly in vain, (could he have time to study and correct every one's particular defects and wrong inclinations) when the lad was to be left to himself, or the prevailing infection of his fellows, the greatest part of the four-and-twenty hours.

But fathers, observing that fortune is often most successfully courted by bold and bustling men, are glad to see their sons pert and forward betimes; take it for a happy omen that they will be thriving men, and look on the tricks they play their schoolfellows, or learn from them, as a proficiency in the art of living, and making their way through the world. But I must take the liberty to say, that he that lays the foundation of his son's fortune in virtue and good breeding, takes the only sure and warrantable way. And it is not the waggeries or cheats practised among schoolboys, it is not their roughness one to another, nor the well-laid plots of robbing an orchard together, that makes an able man; but the principles of justice, generosity, and sobriety, joined with observation and industry, qualities which I judge schoolboys do not learn much of one another. And if a young gentleman, bred at home, be not taught more of them than he could learn at school, his father has made a very ill choice of a tutor. Take a boy from the top of a grammar-school, and one of the same age, bred as he should be in his father's family, and bring them into good company together; and then see which of the two will have the more manly carriage, and address himself with the more becoming assurance to strangers. Here I imagine the schoolboy's confidence will either fail or discredit him; and if it be such as fits him only for the conversation of boys, he had better be without it.

Vice, if we may believe the general complaint, ripens so fast now-a-days, and runs up to seed so early in young people, that it is impossible to keep a lad from the spreading contagion, if you will venture him abroad in the herd, and trust to chance, or his own inclination, for the choice of his company at school. By what fate vice has so thriven amongst us these few years past, and by what hands it has been nursed up into so uncontrolled a dominion, I shall leave to others to inquire. I wish that those who complain of the great decay of Christian piety and virtue every where, and of learning and acquired improvements in the gentry of this generation, would consider how to retrieve them in the next. This I am sure, that, if the foundation of it be not laid in the education and principling of the youth, all other endeavours will be in vain. And if the innocence, sobriety, and industry of those who are coming up be not taken care of and preserved, it will be ridiculous to expect, that those who are to succeed next on the stage should abound in that virtue, ability, and learning, which has hitherto made England considerable in the world. Debauchery sinks the courage of men; and when dissoluteness has eaten out the sense of true honour, bravery seldom stays long after it. And I think it impossible to find an instance of any nation, however renowned for their valour, who ever kept their credit in arms, or made themselves redoubtable amongst their neighbours, after corruption had once broke through, and dissolved the restraint of discipline; and vice was grown to such a head, that it durst show itself barefaced, without being out of countenance.

It is virtue then, direct virtue, which is the hard and valuable part to be aimed at in education; and not a forward pertness, or any little arts of shifting. All other considerations and accomplishments should give way, and be postponed, to this. This is the solid and substantial good, which tutors should not only read lectures, and talk of; but the labour and art of education should furnish the mind with, and fasten there, and never cease till the young man had a true relish of it, and placed his strength, his glory, and his pleasure in it.

The more this advances, the easier way will be made for other accomplishments in their turns. For he that is brought to submit to virtue, will not be refractory, or resty, in any thing that becomes him. And therefore I cannot but prefer breeding of a young gentleman at home in his father's sight, under a good governor, as much the

best and safest way to this great and main end of education; when it can be had, and is ordered as it should be.
Gentlemen's houses are seldom without variety of company: they should use their sons to all the strange faces
that come there, and engage them in conversation with
men of parts and breeding, as soon as they are capable
of it. And why those, who live in the country, should not
take them with them, when they make visits of civility
to their neighbours, I know not: this I am sure, a father
that breeds his son at home, has the opportunity to have
him more in his own company, and there give him what
encouragement he thinks fit; and can keep him better
from the taint of servants, and the meaner sort of people,
than is possible to be done abroad. But what shall be
resolved in the case, must in great measure be left to the
parents, to be determined by their circumstances and con-
veniencies. Only I think it the worst sort of good husbandry for a father not to strain himself a little for his
son's breeding; which, let his condition be what it will, is
the best portion he can leave him. But if, after all, it shall
be thought by some that the breeding at home has too
little company, and that at ordinary schools not such as it
should be for a young gentleman, I think there might be
ways found out to avoid the inconveniencies on the one
side and the other.

§ 71.   Having under consideration how great the influence of company is, and how prone we are all, especially
children, to imitation; I must here take the liberty to
mind parents of this one thing, viz. that he that will have
his son have a respect for him and his orders, must himself have a great reverence for his son. "Maxima debetur
pueris reverentia." [1] You must do nothing before him,
which you would not have him imitate. If any thing

[1] See Introduction, p. 4—P. G.

escape you, which you would have pass for a fault in him, he will be sure to shelter himself under your example, and shelter himself so, as that it will not be easy to come at him to correct it in him the right way. If you punish him for what he sees you practise yourself, he will not think that severity to proceed from kindness in you, or carefulness to amend a fault in him; but will be apt to interpret it the peevishness and arbitrary imperiousness of a father, who, without any ground for it, would deny his son the liberty and pleasures he takes himself. Or if you assume to yourself the liberty you have taken, as a privilege belonging to riper years, to which a child must not aspire, you do but add new force to your example, and recommend the action the more powerfully to him. For you must always remember, that children affect to be men earlier than is thought: and they love breeches, not for their cut, or ease, but because the having them is a mark or a step towards manhood. What I say of the father's carriage before his children, must extend itself to all those who have any authority over them, or for whom he would have them have any respect.

§ 73. 1. None of the things they are to learn should ever be made a burden to them, or imposed on them as a task. Whatever is so proposed presently becomes irksome: the mind takes an aversion to it, though before it were a thing of delight or indifferency. Let a child be but ordered to whip his top at a certain time every day, whether he has or has not a mind to it; let this be but required of him as a duty, wherein he must spend so many hours morning and afternoon, and see whether he will not soon be weary of any play at this rate. Is it not so with grown men? What they do cheerfully of themselves, do they not presently grow sick of, and can no more endure, as soon as they find it is expected of them as a duty? Children have as much a mind to show that they are free, that their own good actions come from themselves, that they are absolute and independent, as any of the proudest of you grown men, think of them as you please.

§ 74. 2. As a consequence of this, they should seldom be put about doing even those things you have got an inclination in them to, but when they have a mind and disposition to it. He that loves reading, writing, music, &c. finds yet in himself certain seasons wherein those things have no relish to him: and, if at that time he forces himself to it, he only pothers and wearies himself to no purpose. So it is with children. This change of temper should be carefully observed in them, and the favourable seasons of aptitude and inclination be heedfully laid hold of: and if they are not often enough forward of themselves, a good disposition should be talked into them, before they be set upon any thing. This I think no hard matter for a discreet tutor to do, who has studied his pupil's temper, and will be at a little pains to fill his head with suitable ideas, such as may make him in love with the present business. By this means a great deal of time and tiring would be saved: for a child will learn three times as much when he is in tune, as he will with double the time and pains, when he goes awkwardly, or is dragged unwillingly to it. If this were minded as it should, children might be permitted to weary themselves with play, and yet have time enough to learn what is suited to the capacity of each age. But no such thing is considered in the ordinary way of education, nor can it well be. That rough discipline of the rod is built upon other principles, has no attraction in it, regards not what humour children are in, nor looks after favourable seasons of inclination. And indeed it would be ridiculous, when compulsion and blows have raised an aversion in the child to his task, to expect he should freely of his own accord leave his play, and with pleasure court the occasions of learning: whereas, were matters ordered right, learning any thing they should be taught might be made as much a recreation to their play, as their play is to their learning. The pains are equal on both sides: nor is it that which troubles them; for they love to be busy, and the change and variety is that which naturally delights them. The only odds is, in that which we call play they act at liberty, and employ their pains (whereof you may observe them never sparing) freely; but what they are to learn, is forced upon them: they are called, compelled, and driven to it. This is that which at first entrance balks and cools them; they want their liberty: get them but to ask their tutor to teach them, as they do often their playfellows, instead of his calling upon them to learn; and they being satisfied that they act as freely in this as they do in other things, they will go on with as much pleasure in it, and it will not differ from their other sports and play. By these ways, carefully pursued, a child may be brought to desire to be taught any thing you have a mind he should learn. The hardest part, I confess, is with the first or eldest; but when once he is set aright, it is easy by him to lead the rest whither one will.

§ 75. Though it be past doubt, that the fittest time for children to learn any thing is when their minds are in tune, and well disposed to it; when neither flagging of spirit, nor intentness of thought upon something else, makes them awkward and averse; yet two things are to be taken care of: 1. that these seasons either not being warily observed, and laid hold on, as often as they return; or else not returning as often as they should; the improvement of the child be not thereby neglected, and so he be let grow into an habitual idleness, and confirmed in this indisposition. 2. That though other things are ill learned when the mind is either indisposed, or otherwise taken up; yet it is of great moment, and worth our endeavours, to teach the mind to get the mastery over itself; and to be able, upon choice, to take itself off from the hot pursuit of one thing, and set itself upon another with facility and delight; or at any time to shake off its sluggishness, and vigorously employ itself about what reason, or the advice of another, shall direct. This is to be done in children, by trying them sometimes, when they are by laziness unbent, or by avocation bent another way, and endeavouring to make them buckle to the thing proposed. If by this means the mind can get an habitual dominion over itself, lay by ideas or business, as occasion requires, and betake itself to new and less acceptable employments, without reluctancy or discomposure, it will be an advantage of more consequence than Latin or logic, or most of those things children are usually required to learn.

§ 76. Children being more active and busy in that age than in any other part of their life, and being indifferent to any thing they can do, so they may be but doing; dancing and scotch-hoppers would be the same thing to them, were the encouragements and discouragements equal. But to things we would have them learn, the great and only discouragement I can observe is, that they are called to it; it is made their business; they are teased and chid about it, and do it with trembling and apprehension; or, when they come willingly to it, are kept too long at it, till they are quite tired: all which intrenches too much on that natural freedom they extremely affect. And it is that liberty alone, which gives the true relish and delight to their ordinary play-games. Turn the tables, and you will find, they will soon change their application; especially if they see the examples of others, whom they esteem and think above themselves. And if the things which they observe others to do, be ordered so that they insinuate themselves into them, as the privilege of an age or condition above theirs; then ambition, and the desire still to get forward, and higher, and to be like those above them, will set them on work, and make them go on with vigour and pleasure; pleasure in what they have begun by their own desire. In which way the enjoyment of their dearly beloved freedom will be no small encouragement to them. To all which, if there be added the satisfaction of credit and reputation, I am apt to think there will need no other spur to excite their application and assiduity, as much as is necessary. I confess, there needs patience and skill, gentleness and attention, and a prudent conduct, to attain this at first. But why have you a tutor, if there needed no pains? But when this is once established, all the rest will follow more easily than in any more severe and imperious discipline. And I think it no hard matter to gain this point; I am sure it will not be, where children have no ill examples set before them. The great danger therefore I apprehend is only from servants, and other ill-ordered children, or such other vicious or foolish people, who spoil children, both by the ill pattern they set before them in their own ill manners, and by giving them together the two things they should never have at once; I mean, vicious pleasures and commendation.

§ 77. As children should very seldom be corrected by blows; so, I think, frequent, and especially passionate chiding, of almost as ill consequence. It lessens the authority of the parents, and the respect of the child: for I bid you still remember, they distinguish early betwixt passion and reason: and as they cannot but have a reverence for what comes from the latter, so they quickly grow into a contempt of the former; or if it causes a present terror, yet it soon wears off; and natural inclination will easily learn to slight such scarecrows, which make a noise, but are not animated by reason. Children being to be restrained by the parents only in vicious (which, in their tender years, are only a few) things, a look or nod only ought to correct them, when they do amiss; or, if words are sometimes to be used, they ought to be grave, kind, and sober, representing the ill, or unbecomingness of the faults, rather than a hasty rating of the child for it, which makes him not sufficiently distinguish whether your dislike be not more directed to him than his fault. Passionate chiding usually carries rough and ill language with it, which has this further ill effect, that it teaches and justifies it in children: and the names that their parents or preceptors give them they will not be ashamed or backward to bestow on others, having so good authority for the use of them.

§ 78. I foresee here it will be objected to me: what then, will you have children never beaten, nor chid, for any fault? this will be to let loose the reins to all kind of disorder. Not so much as is imagined, if a right course has been taken in the first seasoning of their minds, and implanting that awe of their parents above-mentioned. For beating, by constant observation, is found to do little good, where the smart of it is all the punishment is feared or felt in it; for the influence of that quickly wears out with the memory of it. But yet there is one, and but one fault, for which, I think, children should be beaten; and that is obstinacy or rebellion. And in this too I would have it ordered so, if it can be, that the shame of the whipping, and not the pain, should be the greatest part of the punishment. Shame of doing amiss, and deserving chastisement, is the only true restraint belonging to virtue.

The smart of the rod, if shame accompanies it not, soon ceases, and is forgotten, and will quickly, by use, lose its terror. I have known the children of a person of quality kept in awe, by the fear of having their shoes pulled off, as much as others by apprehensions of a rod hanging over them. Some such punishment I think better than beating; for it is shame of the fault, and the disgrace that attends it, that they should stand in fear of, rather than pain, if you would have them have a temper truly ingenuous. But stubbornness, and an obstinate disobedience, must be mastered with force and blows: for this there is no other remedy. Whatever particular action you bid him do, or forbear, you must be sure to see yourself obeyed; no quarter, in this case, no resistance. For when once it comes to be a trial of skill, a contest for mastery betwixt you, as it is, if you command, and he refuses; you must be sure to carry it, whatever blows it costs, if a nod or words will not prevail; unless, for ever after, you intend to live in obedience to your son. A prudent and kind mother, of my acquaintance, was, on such an occasion, forced to whip her little daughter, at her first coming home from nurse, eight times successively, the same morning, before she could master her stubbornness, and obtain a compliance in a very easy and indifferent matter. If she had left off sooner, and stopped at the seventh whipping, she had spoiled the child for ever; and, by her unprevailing blows, only confirmed her refractoriness, very hardly afterwards to be cured: but wisely persisting, till she had bent her mind, and suppled her will, the only end of correction and chastisement, she established her authority thoroughly in the very first occasions, and had ever after a very ready compliance and obedience in all things from her daughter. For, as this was the first time, so, I think, it was the last too she ever struck her.

The pain of the rod, the first occasion that requires it,

continued and increased without leaving off, till it has thoroughly prevailed, should first bend the mind, and settle the parents' authority: and then gravity, mixed with kindness, should for ever after keep it.

This, if well reflected on, would make people more wary in the use of the rod and the cudgel; and keep them from being so apt to think beating the safe and universal remedy, to be applied at random, on all occasions. This is certain, however, if it does no good, it does great harm; if it reaches not the mind, and makes not the will supple, it hardens the offender; and, whatever pain he has suffered for it, it does but endear to him his beloved stubbornness, which has got him this time the victory, and prepares him to contest and hope for it for the future. Thus, I doubt not, but by ill-ordered correction, many have been taught to be obstinate and refractory, who otherwise would have been very pliant and tractable. For, if you punish a child so, as if it were only to revenge the past fault, which has raised your choler; what operation can this have upon his mind, which is the part to be amended? If there were no sturdy humour or wilfulness mixed with his fault, there was nothing in it that required the severity of blows. A kind or grave admonition is enough to remedy the slips of frailty, forgetfulness, or inadvertency, and is as much as they will stand in need of. But, if there were a perverseness in the will, if it were a designed, resolved disobedience, the punishment is not to be measured by the greatness or smallness of the matter wherein it appeared, but by the opposition it carries, and stands in, to that respect and submission that is due to the father's orders; which must always be rigorously exacted, and the blows by pauses laid on, till they reach the mind, and you perceive the signs of a true sorrow, shame, and purpose of obedience.

This, I confess, requires something more than setting children a task, and whipping them without any more ado, if it be not done, and done to our fancy. This requires care, attention, observation, and a nice study of children's tempers, and weighing their faults well, before we come to this sort of punishment. But is not that better than always to have the rod in hand, as the only instrument of government; and, by frequent use of it on all occasions, misapply and render inefficacious this last and useful remedy, where there is need of it? For what else can be expected, when it is promiscuously used upon every little slip? When a mistake in concordance, or a wrong position in verse, shall have the severity of the lash, in a well-tempered and industrious lad, as surely as a wilful crime in an obstinate and perverse offender; how can such a way of correction be expected to do good on the mind, and set that right, which is the only thing to be looked after? and, when set right, brings all the rest that you can desire along with it.

§ 79. Where a wrong bent of the will wants not amendment, there can be no need of blows. All other faults, where the mind is rightly disposed, and refuses not the government and authority of the father or tutor, are but mistakes, and may often be overlooked; or, when they are taken notice of, need no other but the gentle remedies of advice, direction, and reproof; till the repeated and wilful neglect of those shows the fault to be in the mind, and that a manifest perverseness of the will lies at the root of their disobedience. But whenever obstinacy, which is an open defiance, appears, that cannot be winked at, or neglected, but must, in the first instance, be subdued and mastered; only care must be had that we mistake not, and we must be sure it is obstinacy, and nothing else.

§ 80. But since the occasions of punishment, especially beating, are as much to be avoided as may be, I
think it should not be often brought to this point. If the
awe I spoke of be once got, a look will be sufficient in
most cases. Nor indeed should the same carriage, serious-
ness, or application be expected from young children, as
from those of riper growth. They must be permitted, as I
said, the foolish and childish actions suitable to their
years, without taking notice of them; inadvertency, care-
lessness, and gaiety, is the character of that age. I think
the severity I spoke of is not to extend itself to such un-
seasonable restraints; nor is that hastily to be interpreted
obstinacy or wilfulness, which is the natural product of
their age or temper. In such miscarriages they are to be
assisted, and helped towards an amendment, as weak people under a natural infirmity; which, though they are
warned of, yet every relapse must not be counted a perfect
neglect, and they presently treated as obstinate. Faults of
frailty, as they should never be neglected, or let pass without minding; so, unless the will mix with them, they
should never be exaggerated, or very sharply reproved;
but with a gentle hand set right, as time and age permit.
By this means, children will come to see what is in any
miscarriage that is chiefly offensive, and so learn to avoid
it. This will encourage them to keep their wills right,
which is the great business; when they find that it pre-
serves them from any great displeasure; and that in all
their other failings they meet with the kind concern and
help, rather than the anger and passionate reproaches, of
their tutor and parents. Keep them from vice, and vicious
dispositions, and such a kind of behaviour in general will
come, with every degree of their age, as is suitable to that
age, and the company they ordinarily converse with: and
as they grow in years, they will grow in attention and ap-

plication. But that your words may always carry weight and authority with them, if it shall happen, upon any occasion, that you bid him leave off the doing of any even childish things, you must be sure to carry the point, and not let him have the mastery. But yet, I say, I would have the father seldom interpose his authority and command in these cases, or in any other, but such as have a tendency to vicious habits. I think there are better ways of prevailing with them; and a gentle persuasion in reasoning (when the first point of submission to your will is got) will most times do much better.

§ 81. It will perhaps be wondered, that I mention reasoning with children: and yet I cannot but think that the true way of dealing with them. They understand it as early as they do language; and, if I misobserve not, they love to be treated as rational creatures sooner than is imagined. It is a pride should be cherished in them, and, as much as can be, made the greatest instrument to turn them by.

But when I talk of reasoning, I do not intend any other but such as is suited to the child's capacity and apprehension. Nobody can think a boy of three or seven years old should be argued with as a grown man. Long discourses, and philosophical reasonings, at best amaze and confound, but do not instruct, children. When I say, therefore, that they must be treated as rational creatures, I mean, that you should make them sensible, by the mildness of your carriage, and the composure, even in your correction of them, that what you do is reasonable in you, and useful and necessary for them; and that it is not out of caprice, passion, or fancy, that you command or forbid them any thing. This they are capable of understanding; and there is no virtue they should be excited to, nor fault they should be kept from, which I do not think they may be convinced of: but it must be by such reasons as their age and understanding are capable of, and those proposed always in very few and plain words. The foundations on which several duties are built, and the fountains of right and wrong, from which they spring, are not, perhaps, easily to be let into the minds of grown men, not used to abstract their thoughts from common received opinions. Much less are children capable of reasonings from remote principles. They cannot conceive the force of long deductions: the reasons that move them must be obvious, and level to their thoughts, and such as may (if I may so say) be felt and touched. But yet, if their age, temper, and inclinations, be considered, they will never want such motives as may be sufficient to convince them. If there be no other more particular, yet these will always be intelligible, and of force, to deter them from any fault fit to be taken notice of in them, viz. that it will be a discredit and disgrace to them, and displease you.

§ 82.   But, of all the ways whereby children are to be instructed, and their manners formed, the plainest, easiest, and most efficacious, is to set before their eyes the examples of those things you would have them do or avoid. Which, when they are pointed out to them, in the practice of persons within their knowledge, with some reflections on their beauty or unbecomingness, are of more force to draw or deter their imitation than any discourses which can be made to them. Virtues and vices can by no words be so plainly set before their understandings as the actions of other men will show them, when you direct their observation, and bid them view this or that good or bad quality in their practice. And the beauty or uncomeliness of many things, in good and ill breeding, will be better learnt, and make deeper impressions on them, in the examples of others, than from any rules or instructions can be given about them.

This is a method to be used, not only whilst they are young; but to be continued, even as long as they shall be under another's tuition or conduct. Nay, I know not whether it be not the best way to be used by a father, as long as he shall think fit, on any occasion, to reform any thing he wishes mended in his son; nothing sinking so gently, and so deep, into men's minds, as example. And what ill they either overlook, or indulge in themselves, they cannot but dislike, and be ashamed of, when it is set before them in another.

§ 83. It may be doubted concerning whipping, when, as the last remedy, it comes to be necessary; at what times, and by whom it should be done: whether presently upon the committing the fault, whilst it is yet fresh and hot; and whether parents themselves should beat their children. As to the first; I think it should not be done presently, lest passion mingle with it; and so, though it exceed the just proportion, yet it loses of its due weight: for even children discern when we do things in passion. But, as I said before, that has most weight with them, that appears sedately to come from their parents' reason; and they are not without this distinction. Next, if you have any discreet servant capable of it, and has the place of governing your child, (for if you have a tutor, there is no doubt) I think it is best the smart should come more immediately from another's hand, though by the parent's order, who should see it done; whereby the parent's authority will be preserved, and the child's aversion, for the pain it suffers, rather be turned on the person that immediately inflicts it. For I would have a father seldom strike his child, but upon very urgent necessity, and as the last remedy: and then perhaps it will be fit to do it so that the child should not quickly forget it.

§ 84. But, as I said before, beating is the worst, and therefore the last, means to be used in the correction of children; and that only in cases of extremity, after all gentler ways have been tried, and proved unsuccessful; which, if well observed, there will be very seldom any need of blows. For, it not being to be imagined that a child will often, if ever, dispute his father's present command in any particular instance; and the father not interposing his absolute authority, in peremptory rules, concerning either childish or indifferent actions, wherein his son is to have his liberty; or concerning his learning or improvement, wherein there is no compulsion to be used; there remains only the prohibition of some vicious actions, wherein a child is capable of obstinacy, and consequently can deserve beating: and so there will be but very few occasions of that discipline to be used by any one, who considers well, and orders his child's education as it should be. For the first seven years, what vices can a child be guilty of, but lying, or some ill-natured tricks; the repeated commission whereof, after his father's direct command against it, shall bring him into the condemnation of obstinacy, and the chastisement of the rod? If any vicious inclination in him be, in the first appearance and instances of it, treated as it should be, first, with your wonder; and then, if returning again a second time, discountenanced with the severe brow of the father, tutor, and all about him, and a treatment suitable to the state of discredit before-mentioned; and this continued till he be made sensible and ashamed of his fault; I imagine there will be no need of any other correction, nor ever any occasion to come to blows. The necessity of such chastisement is usually the consequence only of former indulgences or neglects. If vicious inclinations were watched from the beginning, and the first irregularities which they caused corrected by those gentler ways, we should seldom have to do with more than one disorder at once; which would be easily set right without any stir or noise, and not require so harsh a discipline as beating. Thus, one by one, as they appeared, they might all be weeded out, without any signs or memory that ever they had been there. But we letting their faults (by indulging and humouring our little ones) grow up, till they are sturdy and numerous, and the deformity of them makes us ashamed and uneasy, we are fain to come to the plough and the harrow; the spade and the pick-axe must go deep to come at the roots, and all the force, skill, and diligence we can use is scarce enough to cleanse the vitiated seed-plat, overgrown with weeds, and restore us the hopes of fruits to reward our pains in its season.

§ 85. This course, if observed, will spare both father and child the trouble of repeated injunctions, and multiplied rules of doing and forbearing. For I am of opinion, that of those actions which tend to vicious habits, (which are those alone that a father should interpose his authority and commands in) none should be forbidden children, till they are found guilty of them. For such untimely prohibitions, if they do nothing worse, do at least so much towards teaching and allowing them, that they suppose that children may be guilty of them, who would possibly be safer in the ignorance of any such faults. And the best remedy to stop them, is, as I have said, to show wonder and amazement at any such action as hath a vicious tendency, when it is first taken notice of in a child. For example, when he is first found in a lie, or any ill-natured trick, the first remedy should be, to talk to him of it as a strange monstrous matter, that it could not be imagined he would have done: and so shame him out of it.

§ 86. It will be (it is like) objected, that whatsoever I fancy of the tractableness of children, and the prevalency

of those softer ways of shame and commendation; yet
there are many, who will never apply themselves to their
books, and to what they ought to learn, unless they are
scourged to it. This, I fear, is nothing but the language
of ordinary schools and fashion, which have never suffered
the other to be tried as it should be, in places where it
could be taken notice of. Why, else, does the learning of
Latin and Greek need the rod, when French and Italian
need it not? Children learn to dance and fence without
whipping: nay, arithmetic, drawing, &c. they apply themselves well enough to, without beating: which would
make one suspect, that there is something strange, unnatural, and disagreeable to that age in the things required in grammar-schools, or in the methods used there,
that children cannot be brought to, without the severity
of the lash, and hardly with that too; or else, that it is a
mistake that those tongues could not be taught them without beating.

§ 87. But let us suppose some so negligent or idle,
that they will not be brought to learn by the gentle ways
proposed (for we must grant that there will be children
found of all tempers); yet it does not thence follow that
the rough discipline of the cudgel is to be used to all. Nor
can any one be concluded unmanageable by the milder
methods of government, till they have been thoroughly
tried upon him; and, if they will not prevail with him to
use his endeavours, and do what is in his power to do, we
make no excuses for the obstinate: blows are the proper
remedies for those: but blows laid on in a way different
from the ordinary. He that wilfully neglects his book, and
stubbornly refuses any thing he can do, required of him
by his father, expressing himself in a positive serious
command, should not be corrected with two or three
angry lashes, for not performing his task, and the same

punishment repeated again and again, upon every the like default: but, when it is brought to that pass, that wilfulness evidently shows itself, and makes blows necessary, I think the chastisement should be a little more sedate, and a little more severe, and the whipping (mingled with admonition between) so continued, till the impressions of it, on the mind, were found legible in the face, voice, and submission of the child, not so sensible of the smart, as of the fault he has been guilty of, and melting in true sorrow under it. If such a correction as this, tried some few times at fit distances, and carried to the utmost severity, with the visible displeasure of the father all the while, will not work the effect, turn the mind, and produce a future compliance; what can be hoped from blows, and to what purpose should they be any more used? Beating, when you can expect no good from it, will look more like the fury of an enraged enemy than the good-will of a compassionate friend; and such chastisement carries with it only provocation, without any prospect of amendment. If it be any father's misfortune to have a son thus perverse and untractable, I know not what more he can do but pray for him. But I imagine, if a right course be taken with children from the beginning, very few will be found to be such; and when there are any such instances, they are not to be the rule for the education of those who are better natured, and may be managed with better usage.

§ 88. If a tutor can be got, that, thinking himself in the father's place, charged with his care, and relishing these things, will at the beginning apply himself to put them in practice, he will afterwards find his work very easy: and you will, I guess, have your son in a little time a greater proficient in both learning and breeding than perhaps you imagine. But let him by no means beat him, at any time, without your consent and direction; at least till you have experience of his discretion and temper. But yet, to keep up his authority with his pupil, besides concealing that he has not the power of the rod, you must be sure to use him with great respect yourself, and cause all your family to do so too. For you cannot expect your son should have any regard for one whom he sees you, or his mother, or others slight.

§ 89. As the father's example must teach the child respect for his tutor; so the tutor's example must lead the child into those actions he would have him do. His practice must by no means cross his precepts, unless he intend to set him wrong. It will be to no purpose for the tutor to talk of the restraint of the passions, whilst any of his own are let loose; and he will in vain endeavour to reform any vice or indecency in his pupil which he allows in himself.

§ 90. In all the whole business of education, there is nothing like to be less hearkened to, or harder to be well observed, than what I am now going to say; and that is, that children should, from their first beginning to talk, have some discreet, sober, nay wise person about them, whose care it should be to fashion them aright, and keep them from all ill, especially the infection of bad company. I think this province requires great sobriety, temperance, tenderness, diligence, and discretion; qualities hardly to be found united in persons that are to be had for ordinary salaries, nor easily to be found any where. As to the charge of it, I think it will be the money best laid out that can be about our children; and therefore, though it may be expensive more than is ordinary, yet it cannot be thought dear. He that at any rate procures his child a good mind, well-principled, tempered to virtue and usefulness, and adorned with civility and good breeding, makes a better purchase for him, than if he had laid out the money for an addition of more earth to his former acres. Spare it in toys and play-games, in silk and ribbons, laces and other useless expenses, as much as you please; but be not sparing in so necessary a part as this. It is not good husbandry to make his fortune rich, and his mind poor.

§ 95. But to return to our method again. Though I have mentioned the severity of the father's brow, and the awe settled thereby in the mind of children when young, as one main instrument, whereby their education is to be managed; yet I am far from being of an opinion, that it should be continued all along to them: whilst they are under the discipline and government of pupilage, I think it should be relaxed, as fast as their age, discretion, and good behaviour could allow it; even to that degree, that a father will do well, as his son grows up, and is capable of it, to talk familiarly with him; nay, ask his advice, and consult with him, about those things wherein he has any knowledge or understanding. By this the father will gain two things, both of great moment. The one is, that it will put serious considerations into his son's thoughts, better than any rules or advices he can give him. The sooner you treat him as a man, the sooner he will begin to be one: and if you admit him into serious discourses sometimes with you, you will insensibly raise his mind above the usual amusements of youth, and those trifling occupations which it is commonly wasted in. For it is easy to observe, that many young men continue longer in the thought and conversation of schoolboys, than otherwise they would, because their parents keep them at that distance, and in that low rank, by all their carriage to them.

§ 96. Another thing of greater consequence, which

you will obtain by such a way of treating him, will be his friendship. Many fathers, though they proportion to their sons liberal allowances, according to their age and condition; yet they keep the knowledge of their estates and concerns from them with as much reservedness as if they were guarding a secret of state from a spy or an enemy. This, if it looks not like jealousy, yet it wants those marks of kindness and intimacy, which a father should show to his son; and, no doubt, often hinders or abates that cheerfulness and satisfaction, wherewith a son should address himself to, and rely upon, his father. And I cannot but often wonder to see fathers, who love their sons very well, yet so order the matter, by a constant stiffness, and a mien of authority and distance to them all their lives, as if they were never to enjoy or have any comfort from those they love best in the world till they have lost them by being removed into another. Nothing cements and establishes friendship and good-will so much as confident communication of concernments and affairs. Other kindnesses, without this, leave still some doubts; but when your son sees you open your mind to him; when he finds that you interest him in your affairs, as things you are willing should, in their turn, come into his hands, he will be concerned for them as for his own; wait his season with patience, and love you in the mean time, who keep him not at the distance of a stranger. This will also make him see, that the enjoyment you have, is not without care; which the more he is sensible of, the less will he envy you the possession, and the more think himself happy under the management of so favourable a friend, and so careful a father. There is scarce any young man of so little thought, or so void of sense, that would not be glad of a sure friend, that he might have recourse to, and freely consult on occasion. The reservedness and distance that fathers keep often deprive their sons of that refuge, which would be of more advantage to them than a hundred rebukes and chidings. Would your son engage in some frolic, or take a vagary; were it not much better he should do it with, than without your knowledge? For since allowances for such things must be made to young men, the more you know of his intrigues and designs, the better will you be able to prevent great mischiefs; and, by letting him see what is like to follow, take the right way of prevailing with him to avoid less inconveniencies. Would you have him open his heart to you, and ask your advice? You must begin to do so with him first, and by your carriage beget that confidence.

§ 97. But whatever he consults you about, unless it lead to some fatal and irremediable mischief, be sure you advise only as a friend of more experience; but with your advice mingle nothing of command or authority, nor more than you would to your equal, or a stranger. That would be to drive him for ever from any farther demanding, or receiving advantage from your counsel. You must consider, that he is a young man, and has pleasures and fancies, which you are passed. You must not expect his inclinations should be just as yours, nor that at twenty he should have the same thoughts you have at fifty. All that you can wish is, that since youth must have some liberty, some out-leaps; they might be with the ingenuity of a son, and under the eye of a father, and then no very great harm can come of it. The way to obtain this, as I said before, is (according as you find him capable) to talk with him about your affairs, propose matters to him familiarly, and ask his advice; and when he ever lights on the right, follow it as his; and if it succeed well, let him have the commendation. This will not at all lessen your authority, but increase his love and esteem of you.

Whilst you keep your estate, the staff will still be in your own hands; and your authority the surer, the more it is strengthened with confidence and kindness. For you have not that power you ought to have over him, till he comes to be more afraid of offending so good a friend than of losing some part of his future expectation.

§ 103. I told you before, that children love liberty; and therefore they should be brought to do the things that are fit for them, without feeling any restraint laid upon them. I now tell you they love something more; and that is dominion: and this is the first original of most vicious habits, that are ordinary and natural. This love of power and dominion shows itself very early, and that in these two things.

§ 104. 1. We see children (as soon almost as they are born, I am sure long before they can speak) cry, grow peevish, sullen, and out of humour, for nothing but to have their wills. They would have their desires submitted to by others; they contend for a ready compliance from all about them, especially from those that stand near or beneath them in age or degree, as soon as they come to consider others with those distinctions.

§ 105. 2. Another thing, wherein they show their love of dominion, is their desire to have things to be theirs; they would have property and possession; pleasing themselves with the power which that seems to give, and the right they thereby have to dispose of them as they please. He that has not observed these two humours working very betimes in children, has taken little notice of their actions: and he who thinks that these two roots of almost all the injustice and contention that so disturb human life are not early to be weeded out, and contrary habits introduced, neglects the proper season to lay the foundations of a good and worthy man. To do this, I imagine, these following things may somewhat conduce.

§ 106. 1. That a child should never be suffered to have what he craves, much less what he cries for, I had said, or so much as speaks for. But that being apt to be misunderstood, and interpreted as if I meant a child should never speak to his parents for any thing, which will perhaps be thought to lay too great a curb on the minds of children, to the prejudice of that love and affection which should be between them and their parents; I shall explain myself a little more particularly. It is fit that they should have liberty to declare their wants to their parents, and that with all tenderness they should be hearkened to, and supplied, at least whilst they are very little. But it is one thing to say, I am hungry; another to say, I would have roast-meat. Having declared their wants, their natural wants, the pain they feel from hunger, thirst, cold, or any other necessity of nature, it is the duty of their parents, and those about them, to relieve them; but children must leave it to the choice and ordering of their parents what they think properest for them, and how much; and must not be permitted to choose for themselves; and say, I would have wine, or white bread; the very naming of it should make them lose it.

§ 107. That which parents should take care of here, is to distinguish between the wants of fancy and those of nature.

Those are truly natural wants, which reason alone, without some other help, is not able to fence against, nor keep from disturbing us. The pains of sickness and hurts, hunger, thirst, and cold, want of sleep and rest, or relaxation of the part wearied with labour, are what all men feel, and the best disposed mind cannot but be sensible of their uneasiness; and therefore ought, by fit applications, to seek their removal, though not with impatience, or over-great haste, upon the first approaches of them, where delay does not threaten some irreparable harm.

The pains that come from the necessities of nature are
monitors to us to beware of greater mischiefs, which they
are the forerunners of; and therefore they must not be
wholly neglected, nor strained too far. But yet, the more
children can be inured to hardships of this kind, by a wise
care to make them stronger in body and mind, the better
it will be for them. I need not here give any caution to
keep within the bounds of doing them good, and to take
care that what children are made to suffer should neither
break their spirits, nor injure their health; parents being
but too apt of themselves to incline, more than they
should, to the softer side.

But, whatever compliance the necessities of nature may
require, the wants of fancy children should never be
gratified in, nor suffered to mention. The very speaking
for any such thing should make them lose it. Clothes,
when they need, they must have; but if they speak for
this stuff, or that colour, they should be sure to go without
it. Not that I would have parents purposely cross the
desires of their children in matters of indifferency: on the
contrary, where their carriage deserves it, and one is sure
it will not corrupt or effeminate their minds, and make
them fond of trifles, I think, all things should be contrived, as much as could be, to their satisfaction, that they
might find the ease and pleasure of doing well. The best
for children is, that they should not place any pleasure in
such things at all, nor regulate their delight by their
fancies; but be indifferent to all that nature has made so.
This is what their parents and teachers should chiefly aim
at: but till this be obtained, all that I oppose here, is the
liberty of asking; which, in these things of conceit, ought
to be restrained by a constant forfeiture annexed to it.

This may perhaps be thought a little too severe, by the
natural indulgence of tender parents: but yet it is no

more than necessary. For since the method I propose is to banish the rod, this restraint of their tongues will be of great use to settle that awe we have elsewhere spoken of, and to keep up in them the respect and reverence due to their parents. Next, it will teach them to keep in, and so master their inclinations. By this means they will be brought to learn the art of stifling their desires, as soon as they rise up in them, when they are easiest to be subdued. For giving vent, gives life and strength to our appetites; and he that has the confidence to turn his wishes into demands, will be but a little way from thinking he ought to obtain them. This I am sure of, every one can more easily bear a denial from himself than from any body else. They should therefore be accustomed betimes to consult and make use of their reason, before they give allowance to their inclinations. It is a great step towards the mastery of our desires, to give this stop to them, and shut them up in silence. This habit, got by children, of staying the forwardness of their fancies, and deliberating whether it be fit or no before they speak, will be of no small advantage to them in matters of greater consequence in the future course of their lives. For that which I cannot too often inculcate is, that whatever the matter be, about which it is conversant, whether great or small, the main (I had almost said only) thing to be considered, in every action of a child, is, what influence it will have upon his mind; what habit it tends to, and is like to settle in him; how it will become him when he is bigger; and, if it be encouraged, whither it will lead him when he is grown up.

My meaning, therefore, is not that children should purposely be made uneasy: this would relish too much of inhumanity and ill-nature, and be apt to infect them with it. They should be brought to deny their appetites; and

their minds, as well as bodies, be made vigorous, easy
and strong, by the custom of having their inclinations in
subjection, and their bodies exercised with hardships; but
all this without giving them any mark or apprehension of
ill-will towards them. The constant loss of what they
craved or carved to themselves should teach them modesty,
submission, and a power to forbear: but the rewarding
their modesty and silence, by giving them what they liked,
should also assure them of the love of those who rigorously exacted this obedience. The contenting themselves
now, in the want of what they wished for, is a virtue, that
another time should be rewarded with what is suited and
acceptable to them; which should be bestowed on them,
as if it were a natural consequence of their good behaviour, and not a bargain about it. But you will lose
your labour, and, what is more, their love and reverence
too, if they can receive from others what you deny them.
This is to be kept very stanch, and carefully to be
watched. And here the servants come again in my way.

§ 108.   If this be begun betimes, and they accustom
themselves early to silence their desires, this useful habit
will settle them; and, as they come to grow up in age
and discretion, they may be allowed greater liberty; when
reason comes to speak in them, and not passion. For
whenever reason would speak, it should be hearkened
to. But, as they should never be heard, when they speak
for any particular thing they would have, unless it be
first proposed to them; so they should always be heard,
and fairly and kindly answered, when they ask after any
thing they would know, and desire to be informed about.
Curiosity should be as carefully cherished in children as
other appetites suppressed.

However strict a hand is to be kept upon all desires
of fancy, yet there is one case wherein fancy must be per-

mitted to speak, and be hearkened to also. Recreation is as necessary as labour or food: but because there can be no recreation without delight, which depends not always on reason, but oftener on fancy, it must be permitted children not only to divert themselves, but to do it after their own fashion, provided it be innocently, and without prejudice to their health; and therefore in this case they should not be denied, if they proposed any particular kind of recreation; though I think, in a well-ordered education, they will seldom be brought to the necessity of asking any such liberty. Care should be taken, that what is of advantage to them, they should always do with delight; and, before they are wearied with one, they should be timely diverted to some other useful employment. But if they are not yet brought to that degree of perfection, that one way of improvement can be made a recreation to them, they must be let loose to the childish play they fancy; which they should be weaned from, by being made surfeited of it: but from things of use, that they are employed in, they should always be sent away with an appetite; at least be dismissed before they are tired, and grow quite sick of it; that so they may return to it again, as to a pleasure that diverts them. For you must never think them set right, till they can find delight in the practice of laudable things; and the useful exercises of the body and mind, taking their turns, make their lives and improvement pleasant in a continued train of recreations, wherein the wearied part is constantly relieved and refreshed. Whether this can be done in every temper, or whether tutors and parents will be at the pains, and have the discretion and patience to bring them to this, I know not; but that it may be done in most children, if a right course be taken to raise in them the desire of credit, esteem, and reputation, I do not at all doubt. And when they have so much true life put into them, they may freely be talked with about what most delights them, and be directed, or let loose to it; so that they may perceive that they are beloved and cherished, and that those under whose tuition they are, are not enemies to their satisfaction. Such a management will make them in love with the hand that directs them, and the virtue they are directed to.

This farther advantage may be made by a free liberty permitted them in their recreations, that it will discover their natural tempers, show their inclinations and aptitudes; and thereby direct wise parents in the choice, both of the course of life and employment they shall design them for, and of fit remedies, in the mean time, to be applied to whatever bent of nature they may observe most likely to mislead any of their children.

§ 109. 2. Children who live together often strive for mastery, whose wills shall carry it over the rest: whoever begins the contest, should be sure to be crossed in it. But not only that, but they should be taught to have all the deference, complaisance, and civility one for the other imaginable. This, when they see it procures them respect, love, and esteem, and that they lose no superiority by it, they will take more pleasure in than in insolent domineering; for so plainly is the other.

The accusations of children one against another, which usually are but the clamours of anger and revenge, desiring aid, should not be favourably received nor hearkened to. It weakens and effeminates their minds to suffer them to complain: and if they endure sometimes crossing or pain from others, without being permitted to think it strange or intolerable, it will do them no harm to learn sufferance, and harden them early. But, though you give no countenance to the complaints of the querulous, yet take care to curb the insolence and ill-nature of the injurious. When you observe it yourself, reprove it before the injured party: but if the complaint be of something really worth your notice and prevention another time, then reprove the offender by himself alone, out of sight of him that complained, and make him go and ask pardon, and make reparation. Which coming thus, as it were, from himself, will be the more cheerfully performed, and more kindly received, the love strengthened between them, and a custom of civility grow familiar amongst your children.

§ 110. 3. As to having and possessing of things, teach them to part with what they have, easily and freely to their friends; and let them find by experience, that the most liberal has always most plenty, with esteem and commendation to boot, and they will quickly learn to practise it. This, I imagine, will make brothers and sisters kinder and civiller to one another, and consequently to others, than twenty rules about good manners, with which children are ordinarily perplexed and cumbered. Covetousness, and the desire of having in our possession, and under our dominion, more than we have need of, being the root of all evil, should be early and carefully weeded out; and the contrary quality, or a readiness to impart to others, implanted. This should be encouraged by great commendation and credit, and constantly taking care, that he loses nothing by his liberality. Let all the instances he gives of such freeness be always repaid, and with interest; and let him sensibly perceive that the kindness he shows to others is no ill husbandry for himself; but that it brings a return of kindness, both from those that receive it, and those who look on. Make this a contest among children, who shall outdo one another this way. And by this means, by a constant practice, children having made it easy to themselves to part with what they have, good-nature may be settled in them into an habit, and they may take pleasure, and pique themselves in being kind, liberal, and civil to others.

If liberality ought to be encouraged, certainly great care is to be taken that children transgress not the rules of justice: and whenever they do, they should be set right; and, if there be occasion for it, severely rebuked.

Our first actions being guided more by self-love than reason or reflection, it is no wonder that in children they should be very apt to deviate from the just measures of right and wrong, which are in the mind the result of improved reason and serious meditation. This the more they are apt to mistake, the more careful guard ought to be kept over them, and every the least slip in this great social virtue taken notice of and rectified; and that in things of the least weight and moment, both to instruct their ignorance, and prevent ill habits, which, from small beginnings, in pins and cherry-stones, will, if let alone, grow up to higher frauds, and be in danger to end at last in downright hardened dishonesty. The first tendency to any injustice that appears must be suppressed with a show of wonder and abhorrency in the parents and governors. But because children cannot well comprehend what injustice is, till they understand property, and how particular persons come by it, the safest way to secure honesty, is to lay the foundations of it early in liberality, and an easiness to part with to others whatever they have, or like, themselves. This may be taught them early, before they have language and understanding enough to form distinct notions of property, and to know what is theirs by a peculiar right exclusive of others. And since children seldom have any thing but by gift, and that for the most part from their parents, they may be at first taught not to take or keep any thing, but what is given them by those whom they take to have a power over it; and, as their capacities enlarge, other rules and cases of justice, and rights concerning "meum" and "tuum," may be proposed and inculcated. If any act of injustice in them appears to proceed, not from mistake, but perverseness in their wills, when a gentle rebuke and shame will not reform this irregular and covetous inclination, rougher remedies must be applied: and it is but for the father or tutor to take and keep from them something that they value, and think their own; or order somebody else to do it; and by such instances make them sensible, what little advantage they are like to make, by possessing themselves unjustly of what is another's, whilst there are in the world stronger and more men than they. But if an ingenuous detestation of this shameful vice be but carefully and early instilled into them, as I think it may, that is the true and genuine method to obviate this crime; and will be a better guard against dishonesty than any considerations drawn from interest; habits working more constantly, and with greater facility, than reason: which, when we have most need of it, is seldom fairly consulted, and more rarely obeyed.

§ 111. Crying is a fault that should not be tolerated in children; not only for the unpleasant and unbecoming noise it fills the house with, but for more considerable reasons, in reference to the children themselves; which is to be our aim in education.

Their crying is of two sorts; either stubborn and domineering, or querulous and whining.

1. Their crying is very often a striving for mastery, and an open declaration of their insolence or obstinacy: when they have not the power to obtain their desire, they will, by their clamour and sobbing, maintain their title and right to it. This is an avowed continuing of their claim,

and a sort of remonstrance against the oppression and injustice of those who deny them what they have a mind to.

§ 112. 2. Sometimes their crying is the effect of pain or true sorrow, and a bemoaning themselves under it.

These two, if carefully observed, may, by the mien, looks, and actions, and particularly by the tone of their crying, be easily distinguished; but neither of them must be suffered, much less encouraged.

1. The obstinate or stomachful crying should by no means be permitted; because it is but another way of flattering their desires, and encouraging those passions, which it is our main business to subdue: and if it be as often it is, upon the receiving any correction, it quite defeats all the good effects of it; for any chastisement, which leaves them in this declared opposition, only serves to make them worse. The restraints and punishments laid on children are all misapplied and lost, as far as they do not prevail over their wills, teach them to submit their passions, and make their minds supple and pliant to what their parents' reason advises them now, and so prepare them to obey what their own reason shall advise hereafter. But if, in any thing wherein they are crossed, they may be suffered to go away crying, they confirm themselves in their desires, and cherish the ill-humour, with a declaration of their right, and a resolution to satisfy their inclinations the first opportunity. This therefore is another argument against the frequent use of blows: for, whenever you come to that extremity, it is not enough to whip or beat them; you must do it, till you find you have subdued their minds; till with submission and patience they yield to the correction; which you shall best discover by their crying, and their ceasing from it upon your bidding. Without this, the beating of children

is but a passionate tyranny over them: and it is mere cruelty, and not correction, to put their bodies in pain, without doing their minds any good. As this gives us a reason why children should seldom be corrected, so it also prevents their being so. For if, whenever they are chastised, it were done thus without passion, soberly and yet effectually too, laying on the blows and smart, not furiously and all at once, but slowly, with reasoning between, and with observation how it wrought, stopping when it had made them pliant, penitent, and yielding; they would seldom need the like punishment again, being made careful to avoid the fault that deserved it. Besides, by this means, as the punishment would not be lost, for being too little, and not effectual; so it would be kept from being too much, if we gave off as soon as we perceived that it reached the mind, and that was bettered. For, since the chiding or beating of children should be always the least that possibly may be, that which is laid on in the heat of anger seldom observes that measure; but is commonly more than it should be, though it prove less than enough.

§ 113. 2. Many children are apt to cry, upon any little pain they suffer; and the least harm that befalls them puts them into complaints and bawling. This few children avoid: for it being the first and natural way to declare their sufferings or wants, before they can speak, the compassion that is thought due to that tender age foolishly encourages, and continues it in them long after they can speak. It is the duty, I confess, of those about children to compassionate them, whenever they suffer any hurt; but not to show it in pitying them. Help and ease them the best you can, but by no means bemoan them. This softens their minds, and makes them yield to the little harms that happen to them; whereby they sink deeper into that part which alone feels, and make larger wounds there, than otherwise they would. They should be hardened against all sufferings, especially of the body, and have no tenderness but what rises from an ingenuous shame and a quick sense of reputation. The many inconveniencies this life is exposed to require we should not be too sensible of every little hurt. What our minds yield not to, makes but a slight impression, and does us but very little harm; it is the suffering of our spirits that gives and continues the pain. This brawniness and insensibility of mind, is the best armour we can have against the common evils and accidents of life; and being a temper that is to be got by exercise and custom, more than any other way, the practice of it should be begun betimes, and happy is he that is taught it early. That effeminacy of spirit, which is to be prevented or cured, and which nothing, that I know, so much increases in children as crying; so nothing, on the other side, so much checks and restrains, as their being hindered from that sort of complaining. In the little harms they suffer, from knocks and falls, they should not be pitied for falling, but bid do so again; which, besides that it stops their crying, is a better way to cure their heedlessness, and prevent their tumbling another time, than either chiding or bemoaning them. But, let the hurts they receive be what they will, stop their crying, and that will give them more quiet and ease at present, and harden them for the future.

§ 118. Curiosity in children (which I had occasion just to mention, § 108) is but an appetite after knowledge, and therefore ought to be encouraged in them, not only as a good sign, but as the great instrument nature has provided, to remove that ignorance they were born with, and which without this busy inquisitiveness will make them dull and useless creatures. The ways to encourage it, and keep it active and busy, are, I suppose, these following:

1. Not to check or discountenance any inquiries he shall make, nor suffer them to be laughed at; but to answer all his questions, and explain the matters he desires to know, so as to make them as much intelligible to him, as suits the capacity of his age and knowledge. But confound not his understanding with explications or notions that are above it, or with the variety or number of things that are not to his present purpose. Mark what it is his mind aims at in the question, and not what words he expresses it in: and, when you have informed and satisfied him in that, you shall see how his thoughts will enlarge themselves, and how by fit answers he may be led on farther than perhaps you could imagine. For knowledge is grateful to the understanding, as light to the eyes: children are pleased and delighted with it exceedingly, especially if they see that their inquiries are regarded, and that their desire of knowing is encouraged and commended. And I doubt not but one great reason, why many children abandon themselves wholly to silly sports, and trifle away all their time insipidly, is, because they have found their curiosity baulked, and their inquiries neglected. But had they been treated with more kindness and respect, and their questions answered, as they should, to their satisfaction, I doubt not but they would have taken more pleasure in learning, and improving their knowledge, wherein there would be still newness and variety, which is what they are delighted with, than in returning over and over to the same play and playthings.

§ 119. 2. To this serious answering their questions, and informing their understandings in what they desire, as if it were a matter that needed it, should be added some peculiar ways of commendation. Let others, whom they esteem, be told before their faces of the knowledge they have in such and such things; and since we are all, even from our cradles, vain and proud creatures, let their vanity be flattered with things that will do them good; and let their pride set them on work on something which may turn to their advantage. Upon this ground you shall find, that there cannot be a greater spur to the attaining what you would have the elder learn and know himself, than to set him upon teaching it his younger brothers and sisters.

§ 120.   3. As children's inquiries are not to be slighted, so also great care is to be taken, that they never receive deceitful and illuding answers. They easily perceive when they are slighted or deceived, and quickly learn the trick of neglect, dissimulation, and falsehood, which they observe others to make use of. We are not to intrench upon truth in any conversation, but least of all with children; since, if we play false with them, we not only deceive their expectation, and hinder their knowledge, but corrupt their innocence, and teach them the worst of vices. They are travellers newly arrived in a strange country, of which they know nothing: we should therefore make conscience not to mislead them. And though their questions seem sometimes not very material, yet they should be seriously answered; for however they may appear to us (to whom they are long since known) inquiries not worth the making, they are of moment to those who are wholly ignorant. Children are strangers to all we are acquainted with; and all the things they meet with, are at first unknown to them, as they once were to us: and happy are they who meet with civil people, that will comply with their ignorance, and help them to get out of it.

If you or I now should be set down in Japan, with all

our prudence and knowledge about us, a conceit whereof makes us perhaps so apt to slight the thoughts and inquiries of children; should we, I say, be set down in Japan, we should, no doubt, (if we would inform ourselves of what is there to be known) ask a thousand questions, which, to a supercilious or inconsiderate Japanese, would seem very idle and impertinent; though to us they would be very material, and of importance to be resolved; and we should be glad to find a man so complaisant and courteous, as to satisfy our demands, and instruct our ignorance.

When any new thing comes in their way, children usually ask the common question of a stranger, What is it? whereby they ordinarily mean nothing but the name; and therefore to tell them how it is called, is usually the proper answer to that demand. The next question usually is, What is it for? And to this it should be answered truly and directly: the use of the thing should be told, and the way explained, how it serves to such a purpose, as far as their capacities can comprehend it; and so of any other circumstances they shall ask about it; not turning them going, till you have given them all the satisfaction they are capable of, and so leading them by your answers into farther questions. And perhaps to a grown man such conversation will not be altogether so idle and insignificant, as we are apt to imagine. The native and untaught suggestions of inquisitive children do often offer things that may set a considering man's thoughts on work. And I think there is frequently more to be learned from the unexpected questions of a child, than the discourses of men, who talk in a road, according to the notions they have borrowed, and the prejudices of their education.

§ 121. 4. Perhaps it may not sometimes be amiss to excite their curiosity, by bringing strange and new things in their way, on purpose to engage their inquiry, and give them occasion to inform themselves about them; and if by chance their curiosity leads them to ask what they should not know, it is a great deal better to tell them plainly, that it is a thing that belongs not to them to know, than to pop them off with a falsehood, or a frivolous answer.

§ 125. This is what I propose, if it be idleness, not from his general temper, but a peculiar or acquired aversion to learning, which you must be careful to examine and distinguish. But, though you have your eyes upon him, to watch what he does with the time which he has at his own disposal, yet you must not let him perceive that you, or any body else do so; for that may hinder him from following his own inclination, which he being full of, and not daring, for fear of you, to prosecute what his head and heart are set upon, he may neglect all other things, which then he relishes not, and so may seem to be idle and listless; when, in truth, it is nothing but being intent on that, which the fear of your eye or knowledge keeps him from executing. To be clear in this point, the observation must be made when you are out of the way, and he not so much as under the restraint of a suspicion that any body has an eye upon him. In those seasons of perfect freedom, let somebody you can trust mark how he spends his time, whether he inactively loiters it away, when, without any check, he is left to his own inclination. Thus, by his employing of such times of liberty, you will easily discern whether it be listlessness in his temper, or aversion to his book, that makes him saunter away his time of study.

§ 126. If some defect in his constitution has cast a damp on his mind, and he be naturally listless and dreaming, this unpromising disposition is none of the easiest to be dealt with; because, generally carrying with it an unconcernedness for the future, it wants the two great springs of action, foresight and desire; which, how to plant and increase, where nature has given a cold and contrary temper, will be the question. As soon as you are satisfied that this is the case, you must carefully inquire whether there be nothing he delights in; inform yourself what it is he is most pleased with; and if you can find any particular tendency his mind hath, increase it all you can, and make use of that to set him on work, and to excite his industry. If he loves praise, or play, or fine clothes, &c. or, on the other side, dreads pain, disgrace, or your displeasure, &c. whatever it be that he loves most, except it be sloth, (for that will never set him on work) let that be made use of to quicken him, and make him bestir himself: for in this listless temper you are not to fear an excess of appetite (as in all other cases) by cherishing it. It is that which you want, and therefore must labour to raise and increase; for, where there is no desire, there will be no industry.

§ 127. If you have not hold enough upon him this way, to stir up vigour and activity in him, you must employ him in some constant bodily labour, whereby he may get an habit of doing something: the keeping him hard to some study were the better way to get him an habit of exercising and applying his mind. But because this is an invisible attention, and nobody can tell when he is, or is not idle at it, you must find bodily employments for him, which he must be constantly busied in, and kept to; and, if they have some little hardship and shame in them, it may not be the worse, that they may the sooner weary him, and make him desire to return to his book: but be sure, when you exchange his book for his other labour, set him such a task, to be done in such a time, as may allow him no opportunity to be idle. Only, after you have by this way brought him to be attentive and industrious at his book, you may, upon his despatching his study within the time set him, give him, as a reward, some respite from his other labour; which you may diminish, as you find him grow more and more steady in his application; and, at last, wholly take off, when his sauntering at his book is cured.

§ 128. We formerly observed, that variety and freedom was that which delighted children, and recommended their plays to them; and that therefore their book, or any thing we would have them learn, should not be enjoined them as business. This their parents, tutors, and teachers, are apt to forget; and their impatience to have them busied in what is fit for them to do, suffers them not to deceive them into it: but, by the repeated injunctions they meet with, children quickly distinguish between what is required of them and what not. When this mistake has once made his book uneasy to him, the cure is to be applied at the other end. And since it will be then too late to endeavour to make it a play to him, you must take the contrary course; observe what play he is most delighted with; enjoin that, and make him play so many hours every day, not as a punishment for playing, but as if it were the business required of him. This, if I mistake not, will, in a few days, make him so weary of his most beloved sport, that he will prefer his book, or any thing, to it, especially if it may redeem him from any part of the task of play is set him; and he may be suffered to employ some part of the time destined to his task of play in his book, or such other exercise as is really useful to him. This I at least think a better cure than that forbidding (which usually increases the desire) or any other punishment should be made use of to remedy it; for, when you have once glutted his appetite, (which may safely be done in all things but eating and drinking) and made him surfeit of what you would have him avoid, you have put into him a principle of aversion, and you need not so much fear afterwards his longing for the same thing again.

§ 129. This, I think, is sufficiently evident, that children generally hate to be idle: all the care then is that their busy humour should be constantly employed in something of use to them; which if you will attain, you must make what you would have them do, a recreation to them, and not a business. The way to do this, so that they may not perceive you have any hand in it, is this proposed here, viz. to make them weary of that which you would not have them do, by enjoining and making them, under some pretence or other, do it till they are surfeited. For example; Does your son play at top and scourge too much? Enjoin him to play so many hours every day, and look that he do it; and you shall see he will quickly be sick of it, and willing to leave it. By this means, making the recreations you dislike a business to him, he will of himself, with delight, betake himself to those things you would have him do, especially if they be proposed as rewards for having performed his task in that play which is commanded him. For, if he be ordered every day to whip his top, so long as to make him sufficiently weary, do you not think he will apply himself with eagerness to his book, and wish for it, if you promise it him as a reward of having whipped his top lustily, quite out all the time that is set him? Children, in the things they do, if they comport with their age, find little difference, so they may be doing: the esteem they have for one thing above another, they borrow from others; so that what those about them make to be a reward to them, will really be so. By this art, it is in their governor's choice, whether

scotch-hoppers shall reward their dancing, or dancing
their scotch-hoppers; whether peg-top, or reading, playing at trap, or studying the globes, shall be more acceptable and pleasing to them; all that they desire being to
be busy, and busy, as they imagine, in things of their own
choice, and which they receive as favours from their parents, or others for whom they have a respect, and with
whom they would be in credit. A set of children thus
ordered, and kept from the ill example of others, would,
all of them, I suppose, with as much earnestness and delight learn to read, write, and what else one would have
them, as others do their ordinary plays: and the eldest
being thus entered, and this made the fashion of the
place, it would be as impossible to hinder them from
learning the one, as it is ordinarily to keep them from the
other.

§ 130. Play-things, I think, children should have, and
of divers sorts; but still to be in the custody of their tutors, or somebody else, whereof the child should have in
his power but one at once, and should not be suffered to
have another, but when he restored that: this teaches
them, betimes, to be careful of not losing or spoiling the
things they have; whereas plenty and variety, in their
own keeping, makes them wanton and careless, and
teaches them from the beginning to be squanderers and
wasters. These, I confess, are little things, and such as
will seem beneath the care of a governor; but nothing
that may form children's minds is to be overlooked and
neglected; and whatsoever introduces habits, and settles
customs in them, deserves the care and attention of their
governors, and is not a small thing in its consequences.

§ 131. Lying is so ready and cheap a cover for any
miscarriage, and so much in fashion amongst all sorts of
people, that a child can hardly avoid observing the use

is made of it on all occasions, and so can scarce be kept, without great care, from getting into it. But it is so ill a quality, and the mother of so many ill ones, that spawn from it, and take shelter under it, that a child should be brought up in the greatest abhorrence of it imaginable: it should be always (when occasionally it comes to be mentioned) spoken of before him with the utmost detestation, as a quality so wholly inconsistent with the name and character of a gentleman, that nobody of any credit can bear the imputation of a lie; a mark that is judged the utmost disgrace, which debases a man to the lowest degree of a shameful meanness, and ranks him with the most contemptible part of mankind, and the abhorred rascality; and is not to be endured in any one, who would converse with people of condition, or have any esteem or reputation in the world. The first time he is found in a lie, it should rather be wondered at, as a monstrous thing in him, than reproved as an ordinary fault. If that keeps him not from relapsing, the next time he must be sharply rebuked, and fall into the state of great displeasure of his father and mother, and all about him, who take notice of it. And if this way work not the cure, you must come to blows; for, after he has been thus warned, a premeditated lie must always be looked upon as obstinacy, and never be permitted to escape unpunished.

§ 132. Children, afraid to have their faults seen in their naked colours, will, like the rest of the sons of Adam, be apt to make excuses. This is a fault usually bordering upon, and leading to untruth, and is not to be indulged in them; but yet it ought to be cured rather with shame than roughness. If, therefore, when a child is questioned for any thing, his first answer be an excuse, warn him soberly to tell the truth; and then, if he persists to shuffle

it off with a falsehood, he must be chastised; but, if he
directly confess, you must commend his ingenuity, and
pardon the fault, be it what it will; and pardon it so, that
you never so much as reproach him with it, or mention it
to him again: for, if you would have him in love with
ingenuity, and by a constant practice make it habitual to
him, you must take care that it never procure him the
least inconvenience; but, on the contrary, his own con-
fession, bringing always with it perfect impunity, should
be, besides, encouraged by some marks of approbation.
If his excuse be such at any time, that you cannot prove
it to have any falsehood in it, let it pass for true, and be
sure not to show any suspicion of it. Let him keep up his
reputation with you as high as is possible; for, when once
he finds he has lost that, you have lost a great and your
best hold upon him. Therefore let him not think he has
the character of a liar with you, as long as you can avoid
it without flattering him in it. Thus some slips in truth
may be overlooked. But, after he has once been corrected
for a lie, you must be sure never after to pardon it in him,
whenever you find, and take notice to him, that he is
guilty of it: for it being a fault which he has been forbid,
and may, unless he be wilful, avoid, the repeating of it
is perfect perverseness, and must have the chastisement
due to that offence.

§ 133. This is what I have thought concerning the
general method of educating a young gentleman; which,
though I am apt to suppose may have some influence on
the whole course of his education, yet I am far from
imagining it contains all those particulars which his growing years, or peculiar temper, may require. But this being
premised in general, we shall, in the next place, descend
to a more particular consideration of the several parts of
his education.

§ 134. That which every gentleman (that takes any care of his education) desires for his son, besides the estate he leaves him, is contained (I suppose) in these four things, virtue, wisdom, breeding, and learning. I will not trouble myself whether these names do not some of them sometimes stand for the same thing, or really include one another. It serves my turn here to follow the popular use of these words, which, I presume, is clear enough to make me be understood, and I hope there will be no difficulty to comprehend my meaning.

§ 135. I place virtue as the first and most necessary of those endowments that belong to a man or a gentleman, as absolutely requisite to make him valued and beloved by others, acceptable or tolerable to himself. Without that, I think, he will be happy neither in this, nor the other world.

§ 136. As the foundation of this, there ought very early to be imprinted on his mind a true notion of God, as of the independent Supreme Being, Author and Maker of all things, from whom we receive all our good, who loves us, and gives us all things: and, consequent to this, instil into him a love and reverence of this Supreme Being. This is enough to begin with, without going to explain this matter any farther, for fear, lest by talking too early to him of spirits, and being unseasonably forward to make him understand the incomprehensible nature of that infinite Being, his head be either filled with false, or perplexed with unintelligible notions of him. Let him only be told upon occasion, that God made and governs all things, hears and sees every thing, and does all manner of good to those that love and obey him. You will find, that, being told of such a God, other thoughts will be apt to rise up fast enough in his mind about him; which, as you observe them to have any mistakes, you

must set right. And I think it would be better, if men
generally rested in such an idea of God, without being
too curious in their notions about a Being, which all
must acknowledge incomprehensible; whereby many, who
have not strength and clearness of thought to distinguish
between what they can, and what they cannot know, run
themselves into superstition or atheism, making God like
themselves, or (because they cannot comprehend any
thing else) none at all. And I am apt to think the keeping
children constantly morning and evening to acts of de-
votion to God, as to their Maker, Preserver, and Bene-
factor, in some plain and short form of prayer, suitable
to their age and capacity, will be of much more use to
them in religion, knowledge, and virtue, than to distract
their thoughts with curious inquiries into his inscrutable
essence and being.

§ 137. Having by gentle degrees, as you find him
capable of it, settled such an idea of God in his mind,
and taught him to pray to him, and praise him as the
Author of his being, and of all the good he does or can
enjoy, forbear any discourse of other spirits, till the mention of them coming in his way, upon occasion hereafter
to be set down, and his reading the Scripture-history, put
him upon that inquiry.

§ 138. But even then, and always whilst he is young,
be sure to preserve his tender mind from all impressions
and notions of spirits and goblins, or any fearful apprehensions in the dark. This he will be in danger of from
the indiscretion of servants, whose usual method is to
awe children, and keep them in subjection, by telling
them of raw-head and bloody-bones, and such other
names, as carry with them the ideas of something terrible
and hurtful, which they have reason to be afraid of, when
alone, especially in the dark. This must be carefully pre-

vented; for though by this foolish way they may keep them from little faults, yet the remedy is much worse than the disease; and there are stamped upon their imaginations ideas that follow them with terror and affrightment. Such bugbear thoughts, once got into the tender minds of children, and being set on with a strong impression from the dread that accompanies such apprehensions, sink deep, and fasten themselves so, as not easily, if ever, to be got out again; and, whilst they are there, frequently haunt them with strange visions, making children dastards when alone, and afraid of their shadows and darkness all their lives after.

§ 139. Having laid the foundations of virtue in a true notion of a God, such as the creed wisely teaches, as far as his age is capable, and by accustoming him to pray to him; the next thing to be taken care of, is to keep him exactly to speaking of truth, and by all the ways imaginable inclining him to be good-natured. Let him know, that twenty faults are sooner to be forgiven than the straining of truth, to cover any one by an excuse: and to teach him betimes to love and be good-natured to others, is to lay early the true foundation of an honest man; all injustice generally springing from too great love of ourselves, and too little of others.

This is all I shall say of this matter in general, and is enough for laying the first foundations of virtue in a child. As he grows up, the tendency of his natural inclination must be observed; which, as it inclines him, more than is convenient, on one or the other side, from the right path of virtue, ought to have proper remedies applied; for few of Adam's children are so happy as not to be born with some bias in their natural temper, which it is the business of education either to take off, or counterbalance: but to enter into particulars of this, would be beyond the design

of this short treatise of education. I intend not a discourse
of all the virtues and vices, and how each virtue is to be
attained, and every particular vice by its peculiar remedies cured; though I have mentioned some of the most
ordinary faults, and the ways to be used in correcting
them.

§ 140.   Wisdom I take, in the popular acceptation, for
a man's managing his business ably, and with foresight, in
this world. This is the product of a good natural temper,
application of mind and experience together, and so
above the reach of children. The greatest thing that in
them can be done towards it, is to hinder them, as much
as may be, from being cunning; which, being the ape of
wisdom, is the most distant from it that can be: and, as
an ape, for the likeness it has to a man, wanting what
really should make him so, is by so much the uglier; cunning is only the want of understanding; which, because
it cannot compass its ends by direct ways, would do it by
a trick and circumvention; and the mischief of it is, a
cunning trick helps but once, but hinders ever after. No
cover was ever made either so big, or so fine, as to hide
itself. Nobody was ever so cunning, as to conceal their
being so: and, when they are once discovered, every body
is shy, every body distrustful of crafty men; and all the
world forwardly join to oppose and defeat them: whilst
the open, fair, wise man has every body to make way for
him, and goes directly to his business. To accustom a
child to have true notions of things, and not to be satisfied
till he has them; to raise his mind to great and worthy
thoughts; and to keep him at a distance from falsehood,
and cunning, which has always a broad mixture of falsehood in it; is the fittest preparation of a child for wisdom.
The rest, which is to be learned from time, experience,
and observation, and an acquaintance with men, their

tempers and designs, is not to be expected in the ignorance and inadvertency of childhood, or the inconsiderate heat and unwariness of youth: all that can be done towards it, during this unripe age, is, as I have said, to accustom them to truth and sincerity; to a submission to reason; and, as much as may be, to reflection on their own actions.

§ 141. The next good quality belonging to a gentleman, is good-breeding. There are two sorts of ill-breeding; the one, a sheepish bashfulness; and the other, a misbecoming negligence and disrespect in our carriage; both which are avoided, by duly observing this one rule, Not to think meanly of ourselves, and not to think meanly of others.

§ 142. The first part of this rule must not be understood in opposition to humility, but to assurance. We ought not to think so well of ourselves, as to stand upon our own value; and assume to ourselves a preference before others, because of any advantage we may imagine we have over them; but modestly to take what is offered, when it is our due. But yet we ought to think so well of ourselves, as to perform those actions which are incumbent on, and expected of us, without discomposure or disorder, in whose presence soever we are, keeping that respect and distance which is due to every one's rank and quality. There is often in people, especially children, a clownish shamefacedness before strangers, or those above them; they are confounded in their thoughts, words, and looks, and so lose themselves in that confusion, as not to be able to do any thing, or at least not to do it with that freedom and gracefulness which pleases and makes them acceptable. The only cure for this, as for any other miscarriage, is by use to introduce the contrary habit. But since we cannot accustom ourselves to converse with strangers, and persons of quality, without being in their company, nothing can cure this part of ill-breeding but change and variety of company, and that of persons above us.

§ 143. As the before-mentioned consists in too great a concern how to behave ourselves towards others, so the other part of ill-breeding lies in the appearance of too little care of pleasing or showing respect to those we have to do with. To avoid this these two things are requisite: first, a disposition of the mind not to offend others; and secondly, the most acceptable and agreeable way of expressing that disposition. From the one, men are called civil; from the other, well-fashioned. The latter of these is that decency and gracefulness of looks, voice, words, motions, gestures, and of all the whole outward demeanour, which takes in company, and makes those with whom we may converse easy and well pleased. This is, as it were, the language, whereby that internal civility of the mind is expressed; which, as other languages are, being very much governed by the fashion and custom of every country, must, in the rules and practice of it, be learned chiefly from observation, and the carriage of those who are allowed to be exactly well-bred. The other part, which lies deeper than the outside, is that general good-will and regard for all people, which makes any one have a care not to show, in his carriage, any contempt, disrespect, or neglect of them; but to express, according to the fashion and way of that country, a respect and value for them, according to their rank and condition. It is a disposition of the mind that shows itself in the carriage, whereby a man avoids making any one uneasy in conversation.

I shall take notice of four qualities, that are most directly opposite to this first and most taking of all the social virtues. And from some one of these four it is, that incivility commonly has its rise. I shall set them down, that children may be preserved or recovered from their ill influence.

1. The first is, a natural roughness, which makes a man uncomplaisant to others, so that he has no deference for their inclinations, tempers, or conditions. It is the sure badge of a clown, not to mind what pleases or displeases those he is with; and yet one may often find a man, in fashionable clothes, give an unbounded swing to his own humour, and suffer it to justle or over-run any one that stands in its way, with a perfect indifferency how they take it. This is a brutality that every one sees and abhors, and nobody can be easy with: and therefore this finds no place in any one, who would be thought to have the least tincture of good-breeding. For the very end and business of good-breeding is to supple the natural stiffness, and so soften men's tempers, that they may bend to a compliance, and accommodate themselves to those they have to do with.

2. Contempt, or want of due respect, discovered either in looks, words, or gesture: this, from whomsoever it comes, brings always uneasiness with it; for nobody can contentedly bear being slighted.

3. Censoriousness, and finding fault with others, has a direct opposition to civility. Men, whatever they are, or are not guilty of, would not have their faults displayed, and set in open view and broad daylight, before their own, or other people's eyes. Blemishes affixed to any one, always carry shame with them: and the discovery, or even bare imputation of any defect, is not borne without some uneasiness. Raillery is the most refined way of exposing the faults of others; but, because it is usually done with wit and good language, and gives entertainment to the company, people are led into a mistake, and, where it

keeps within fair bounds, there is no incivility in it: and so the pleasantry of this sort of conversation often introduces it amongst people of the better rank; and such talkers are favourably heard, and generally applauded by the laughter of the bystanders on their side: but they ought to consider, that the entertainment of the rest of the company is at the cost of that one, who is set out in their burlesque colours, who therefore is not without uneasiness, unless the subject, for which he is rallied, be really in itself matter of commendation; for then the pleasant images and representations, which make the raillery, carrying praise as well as sport with them, the rallied person also finds his account, and takes part in the diversion. But, because the nice management of so nice and ticklish a business, wherein a little slip may spoil all, is not every body's talent, I think those, who would secure themselves from provoking others, especially all young people, should carefully abstain from raillery; which, by a small mistake, or any wrong turn, may leave upon the mind of those, who are made uneasy by it, the lasting memory of having been piquantly, though wittily, taunted for something censurable in them.

Besides raillery, contradiction is a kind of censoriousness, wherein ill-breeding often shows itself. Complaisance does not require that we should always admit all the reasonings or relations that the company is entertained with; no, nor silently let pass all that is vented in our hearing. The opposing the opinions, and rectifying the mistakes of others, is what truth and charity sometimes require of us, and civility does not oppose, if it be done with due caution and care of circumstances. But there are some people, that one may observe possessed, as it were, with the spirit of contradiction, that steadily, and without regard to right or wrong, oppose some one, or perhaps every one of the company, whatever they say. This is so visible and outrageous a way of censuring, that nobody can avoid thinking himself injured by it. All opposition to what another man has said, is so apt to be suspected of censoriousness, and is so seldom received without some sort of humiliation, that it ought to be made in the gentlest manner, and softest words can be found; and such as, with the whole deportment, may express no forwardness to contradict. All marks of respect and good-will ought to accompany it, that, whilst we gain the argument, we may not lose the esteem of those that hear us.

4. Captiousness is another fault opposite to civility, not only because it often produces misbecoming and provoking expressions and carriage, but because it is a tacit accusation and reproach of some incivility, taken notice of in those whom we are angry with. Such a suspicion, or intimation, cannot be borne by any one without uneasiness. Besides, one angry body discomposes the whole company, and the harmony ceases upon any such jarring.

The happiness, that all men so steadily pursue, consisting in pleasure, it is easy to see why the civil are more acceptable than the useful. The ability, sincerity, and good intention, of a man of weight and worth, or a real friend, seldom atone for the uneasiness, that is produced by his grave and solid representations. Power and riches, nay virtue itself, are valued only as conducing to our happiness; and therefore he recommends himself ill to another, as aiming at his happiness, who, in the services he does him, makes him uneasy in the manner of doing them. He that knows how to make those he converses with easy, without debasing himself to low and servile flattery, has found the true art of living in the world, and being both welcome and valued every where. Civility therefore is what, in the first place, should with great care be made habitual to children and young people.

§ 144. There is another fault in good manners, and

that is, excess of ceremony, and an obstinate persisting to
force upon another what is not his due, and what he cannot take without folly or shame. This seems rather a
design to expose, than oblige; or, at least, looks like a
contest for mastery; and, at best, is but troublesome, and
so can be no part of good breeding, which has no other
use or end, but to make people easy and satisfied in their
conversation with us. This is a fault few young people
are apt to fall into; but yet, if they are ever guilty of it,
or are suspected to incline that way, they should be told
of it, and warned of this mistaken civility. The thing
they should endeavour and aim at in conversation, should
be to show respect, esteem, and good-will, by paying
to every one that common ceremony and regard, which
is in civility due to them. To do this, without a suspicion
of flattery, dissimulation, or meanness, is a great skill,
which good sense, reason, and good company, can only
teach; but is of so much use in civil life, that it is well
worth the studying.

§ 147. You will wonder, perhaps, that I put learning
last, especially if I tell you I think it the least part. This
may seem strange in the mouth of a bookish man: and
this making usually the chief, if not only bustle and stir
about children, this being almost that alone which is
thought on, when people talk of education, makes it the
greater paradox. When I consider what ado is made
about a little Latin and Greek, how many years are
spent in it, and what a noise and business it makes to no
purpose, I can hardly forbear thinking, that the parents
of children still live in fear of the schoolmaster's rod,
which they look on as the only instrument of education;
as if a language or two were its whole business. How else
is it possible, that a child should be chained to the oar
seven, eight, or ten of the best years of his life, to get a

language or two, which I think might be had at a great deal cheaper rate of pains and time, and be learned almost in playing?

Forgive me, therefore, if I say, I cannot with patience think, that a young gentleman should be put into the herd, and be driven with a whip and scourge, as if he were to run the gantlet through the several classes. "What then, say you, would you not have him write and read?" Not so, not so fast, I beseech you. Reading, and writing, and learning, I allow to be necessary, but yet not the chief business. I imagine you would think him a very foolish fellow, that should not value a virtuous, or a wise man, infinitely before a great scholar. Not but that I think learning a great help to both, in well disposed minds; but yet it must be confessed also, that in others not so disposed, it helps them only to be the more foolish, or worse men. I say this, that, when you consider of the breeding of your son, and are looking out for a schoolmaster, or a tutor, you would not have (as is usual) Latin and logic only in your thoughts. Learning must be had, but in the second place, as subservient only to greater qualities. Seek out somebody, that may know how discreetly to frame his manners: place him in hands, where you may, as much as possible, secure his innocence, cherish and nurse up the good, and gently correct and weed out any bad inclinations, and settle in him good habits. This is the main point; and this being provided for, learning may be had into the bargain; and that, as I think, at a very easy rate, by methods that may be thought on.

§ 148. When he can talk, it is time he should begin to learn to read. But as to this, give me leave here to inculcate again what is very apt to be forgotten, viz. that a great care is to be taken, that it be never made as a busi-

ness to him, nor he look on it as a task. We naturally, as
I said, even from our cradles, love liberty, and have therefore an aversion to many things, for no other reason, but
because they are enjoined us. I have always had a fancy,
that learning might be made a play and recreation to
children; and that they might be brought to desire to be
taught, if it were proposed to them as a thing of honour,
credit, delight, and recreation, or as a reward for doing
something else, and if they were never chid or corrected
for the neglect of it. That which confirms me in this
opinion is, that amongst the Portuguese, it is so much
a fashion and emulation amongst their children to learn
to read and write, that they cannot hinder them from it:
they will learn it one from another, and are as intent on
it as if it were forbid them. I remember, that being at a
friend's house, whose younger son, a child in coats, was
not easily brought to his book (being taught to read at
home by his mother); I advised to try another way than
requiring it of him as his duty. We therefore, in a discourse on purpose amongst ourselves, in his hearing, but
without taking any notice of him, declared, that it was
the privilege and advantage of heirs and elder brothers, to
be scholars; that this made them fine gentlemen, and beloved by every body: and that for younger brothers, it was
a favour to admit them to breeding; to be taught to read
and write was more than came to their share; they might
be ignorant bumpkins and clowns, if they pleased. This
so wrought upon the child, that afterwards he desired to
be taught; would come himself to his mother to learn;
and would not let his maid be quiet, till she heard him
his lesson. I doubt not but some way like this might be
taken with other children; and, when their tempers are
found, some thoughts be instilled into them, that might
set them upon desiring of learning themselves, and make

them seek it, as another sort of play or recreation. But then, as I said before, it must never be imposed as a task, nor made a trouble to them. There may be dice, and playthings, with the letters on them, to teach children the alphabet by playing; and twenty other ways may be found, suitable to their particular tempers, to make this kind of learning a sport to them.

§ 149. Thus children may be cozened into a knowledge of the letters; be taught to read, without perceiving it to be any thing but a sport, and play themselves into that which others are whipped for. Children should not have any thing like work, or serious, laid on them; neither their minds nor bodies will bear it. It injures their healths; and their being forced and tied down to their books, in an age at enmity with all such restraint, has, I doubt not, been the reason why a great many have hated books and learning all their lives after: it is like a surfeit, that leaves an aversion behind, not to be removed.

§ 150. I have therefore thought, that if playthings were fitted to this purpose, as they are usually to none, contrivances might be made to teach children to read, whilst they thought they were only playing. For example: What if an ivory-ball were made like that of the royal oak lottery, with thirty-two sides, or one rather of twenty-four or twenty-five sides; and upon several of those sides pasted on an A, upon several others B, on others C, and on others D? I would have you begin with but these four letters, or perhaps only two at first; and when he is perfect in them, then add another; and so on, till each side having one letter, there be on it the whole alphabet. This I would have others play with before him, it being as good a sort of play to lay a stake who shall first throw an A or B, as who upon dice shall throw six or seven. This being a play amongst you, tempt him not to it,

lest you make it business; for I would not have him understand it is any thing but a play of older people, and
I doubt not but he will take to it of himself. And that
he may have the more reason to think it is a play, that
he is sometimes in favour admitted to; when the play is
done, the ball should be laid up safe out of his reach,
that so it may not, by his having it in his keeping at any
time, grow stale to him.

§ 151. To keep up his eagerness to it, let him think
it a game belonging to those above him: and when by
this means he knows the letters, by changing them into
syllables, he may learn to read, without knowing how he
did so, and never have any chiding or trouble about it,
nor fall out with books, because of the hard usage and
vexation they have caused him. Children, if you observe
them, take abundance of pains to learn several games,
which, if they should be enjoined them, they would abhor
as a task, and business. I know a person of great quality
(more yet to be honoured for his learning and virtue,
than for his rank and high place) who, by pasting on the
six vowels, (for in our language Y is one) on the six sides
of a die, and the remaining eighteen consonants on the
sides of three other dice, has made this a play for his children, that he shall win, who, at one cast, throws most
words on these four dice; whereby his eldest son, yet
in coats, has played himself into spelling, with great
eagerness, and without once having been chid for it, or
forced to it.

§ 153. The letters pasted upon the sides of the dice,
or polygon, were best to be of the size of those of the folio
bible to begin with, and none of them capital letters;
when once he can read what is printed in such letters,
he will not long be ignorant of the great ones: and in the
beginning he should not be perplexed with variety. With

this die also, you might have a play just like the royal-oak, which would be another variety; and play for cherries, or apples, &c.

§ 154. Besides these, twenty other plays might be invented, depending on letters, which those, who like this way, may easily contrive, and get made to this use, if they will. But the four dice abovementioned I think so easy and useful, that it will be hard to find any better, and there will be scarce need of any other.

§ 155. Thus much for learning to read, which let him never be driven to, nor chid for; cheat him into it if you can, but make it not a business for him. It is better it be a year later before he can read, than that he should this way get an aversion to learning. If you have any contests with him, let it be in matters of moment, of truth, and good-nature; but lay no task on him about A B C. Use your skill to make his will supple and pliant to reason: teach him to love credit and commendation; to abhor being thought ill or meanly of, especially by you and his mother; and then the rest will come all easily. But, I think, if you will do that, you must not shackle and tie him up with rules about indifferent matters, nor rebuke him for every little fault, or perhaps some, that to others would seem great ones. But of this I have said enough already.

§ 156. When by these gentle ways he begins to be able to read, some easy pleasant book, suited to his capacity, should be put into his hands, wherein the entertainment that he finds, might draw him on, and reward his pains in reading; and yet not such as should fill his head with perfectly useless trumpery; or lay the principles of vice and folly. To this purpose I think Æsop's Fables the best, which being stories apt to delight and entertain a child, may yet afford useful reflections to a grown man; and if his memory retain them all his life after, he will not repent to find them there, amongst his manly thoughts, and serious business. If his Æsop has pictures in it, it will entertain him much the better, and encourage him to read, when it carries the increase of knowledge with it: for such visible objects children hear talked of in vain, and without any satisfaction, whilst they have no ideas of them; those ideas being not to be had from sounds, but from the things themselves, or their pictures. And therefore, I think, as soon as he begins to spell, as many pictures of animals should be got him as can be found, with the printed names to them, which at the same time will invite him to read, and afford him matter of inquiry and knowledge. Reynard the Fox is another book, I think, may be made use of to the same purpose. And if those about him will talk to him often about the stories he has read, and hear him tell them, it will, besides other advantages, add encouragement and delight to his reading, when he finds there is some use and pleasure in it. These baits seem wholly neglected in the ordinary method; and it is usually long before learners find any use or pleasure in reading, which may tempt them to it, and so take books only for fashionable amusements, or impertinent troubles, good for nothing.

§ 157. The Lord's prayer, the creed, and ten commandments, it is necessary he should learn perfectly by heart; but, I think, not by reading them himself in his primer, but by somebody's repeating them to him, even before he can read. But learning by heart, and learning to read, should not, I think, be mixed, and so one made to clog the other. But his learning to read should be made as little trouble or business to him as might be.

What other books there are in English of the kind of those abovementioned, fit to engage the liking of children, and tempt them to read, I do not know; but am apt to think, that children, being generally delivered over to the method of schools, where the fear of the rod is to inforce, and not any pleasure of the employment to invite, them to learn; this sort of useful books, amongst the number of silly ones that are of all sorts, have yet had the fate to be neglected; and nothing that I know has been considered of this kind out of the ordinary road of the horn-book, primer, psalter, Testament, and Bible.

§ 158. As for the Bible, which children are usually employed in, to exercise and improve their talent in reading, I think the promiscuous reading of it, though by chapters as they lie in order, is so far from being of any advantage to children, either for the perfecting their reading, or principling their religion, that perhaps a worse could not be found. For what pleasure or encouragement can it be to a child, to exercise himself in reading those parts of a book where he understands nothing? And how little are the law of Moses, the Song of Solomon, the prophecies in the Old, and the epistles and apocalypse in the New Testament, suited to a child's capacity? And though the history of the evangelists, and the Acts, have something easier; yet, taken all together, it is very disproportional to the understanding of childhood. I grant, that the principles of religion are to be drawn from thence, and in the words of the scripture; yet none should be proposed to a child, but such as are suited to a child's capacity and notions. But it is far from this to read through the whole Bible, and that for reading's sake. And what an odd jumble of thoughts must a child have in his head, if he have any at all, such as he should have concerning religion, who in his tender age reads all the parts of the Bible indifferently, as the word of God, without any other distinction! I am apt to think, that this, in some

men, has been the very reason why they never had clear
and distinct thoughts of it all their lifetime.

§ 159. And now I am by chance fallen on this subject, give me leave to say, that there are some parts of the
scripture, which may be proper to be put into the hands
of a child to engage him to read; such as are the story of
Joseph and his brethren, of David and Goliath, of David
and Jonathan, &c. and others, that he should be made
to read for his instruction; as that, "What you would
have others do unto you, do you the same unto them;"
and such other easy and plain moral rules, which, being
fitly chosen, might often be made use of, both for reading
and instruction together; and so often read, till they are
thoroughly fixed in his memory; and then afterwards, as
he grows ripe for them, may in their turns, on fit occasions, be inculcated as the standing and sacred rules of
his life and actions. But the reading of the whole scripture indifferently, is what I think very inconvenient for
children, till, after having been made acquainted with
the plainest fundamental parts of it, they have got some
kind of general view of what they ought principally to
believe and practise, which yet, I think, they ought to
receive in the very words of the scripture, and not in such
as men, prepossessed by systems and analogies, are apt in
this case to make use of, and force upon them. Dr. Worthington,[2] to avoid this, has made a catechism, which has
all its answers in the precise words of the scripture, a thing
of good example, and such a sound form of words, as no

[2] John Worthington (1618–1671), Master of Jesus College, Cambridge, until he was replaced in 1660, at the time of the Restoration.
He was close to the Cambridge Platonists in his passion for philosophical theology and disdain for intolerance. His *A Form of Sound
Words: Or a Scripture Catechism; Shewing What a Christian is to
Believe and Practise in Order to Salvation* (1673) appeared post-
humously and was often reprinted.—P. G.

Christian can except against, as not fit for his child to learn. Of this, as soon as he can say the Lord's prayer, creed, and ten commandments by heart, it may be fit for him to learn a question every day, or every week, as his understanding is able to receive, and his memory to retain them. And, when he has this catechism perfectly by heart, so as readily and roundly to answer to any question in the whole book, it may be convenient to lodge in his mind the remaining moral rules, scattered up and down in the Bible, as the best exercise of his memory, and that which may be always a rule to him, ready at hand, in the whole conduct of his life.

§ 160. When he can read English well, it will be seasonable to enter him in writing. And here the first thing should be taught him, is to hold his pen right; and this he should be perfect in, before he should be suffered to put it to paper: for not only children, but any body else, that would do any thing well, should never be put upon too much of it at once, or be set to perfect themselves in two parts of an action at the same time, if they can possibly be separated. I think the Italian way of holding the pen between the thumb and the fore-finger alone may be best; but in this you should consult some good writing-master, or any other person who writes well, and quick. When he has learned to hold his pen right, in the next place he should learn how to lay his paper, and place his arm and body to it. These practices being got over, the way to teach him to write without much trouble, is to get a plate graved with the characters of such a hand as you like best: but you must remember to have them a pretty deal bigger than he should ordinarily write; for every one naturally comes by degrees to write a less hand than he at first was taught, but never a bigger. Such a plate being graved, let several sheets of good writing-paper be printed off with red ink, which he has nothing to do but to go over with a good pen filled with black ink, which will quickly bring his hand to the formation of those characters, being at first showed where to begin, and how to form every letter. And when he can do that well, he must then exercise on fair paper; and so may easily be brought to write the hand you desire.

§ 161. When he can write well, and quick, I think it may be convenient, not only to continue the exercise of his hand in writing, but also to improve the use of it farther in drawing, a thing very useful to a gentleman on several occasions, but especially if he travel, as that which helps a man often to express, in a few lines well put together, what a whole sheet of paper in writing would not be able to represent and make intelligible. How many buildings may a man see, how many machines and habits meet with, the ideas whereof would be easily retained and communicated by a little skill in drawing; which, being committed to words, are in danger to be lost, or at best but ill retained in the most exact descriptions? I do not mean that I would have your son a perfect painter; to be that to any tolerable degree, will require more time than a young gentleman can spare from his other improvements of greater moment; but so much insight into perspective, and skill in drawing, as will enable him to represent tolerably on paper any thing he sees, except faces, may, I think, be got in a little time, especially if he have a genius to it: but where that is wanting, unless it be in the things absolutely necessary, it is better to let him pass them by quietly, than to vex him about them to no purpose: and therefore in this, as in all other things not absolutely necessary, the rule holds, "Nihil invitâ Minervâ." [3]

[3] The full line, from Horace's *Ars poetica*, 385, reads: "*Tu nihil*

§ 162. As soon as he can speak English, it is time for him to learn some other language: this nobody doubts of, when French is proposed. And the reason is, because people are accustomed to the right way of teaching that language, which is by talking it into children in constant conversation, and not by grammatical rules. The Latin tongue would easily be taught the same way, if his tutor, being constantly with him, would talk nothing else to him, and make him answer still in the same language. But because French is a living language, and to be used more in speaking, that should be first learned, that the yet pliant organs of speech might be accustomed to a due formation of those sounds, and he get the habit of pronouncing French well, which is the harder to be done the longer it is delayed.

§ 163. When he can speak and read French well, which in this method is usually in a year or two, he should proceed to Latin, which it is a wonder parents, when they have had the experiment in French, should not think ought to be learned the same way, by talking and reading. Only care is to be taken, whilst he is learning these foreign languages, by speaking and reading nothing else with his tutor, that he do not forget to read English, which may be preserved by his mother, or somebody else, hearing him read some chosen parts of the scripture or other English book, every day.

§ 164. Latin I look upon as absolutely necessary to a gentleman; and indeed custom, which prevails over every thing, has made it so much a part of education, that even those children are whipped to it, and made spend many hours of their precious time uneasily in Latin, who, after

---

invita dices faciesve Minerva" ("You will neither say nor do anything if Minerva is unwilling," i.e., if it goes against your natural inclinations).—P. G.

they are once gone from school, are never to have more to do with it, as long as they live. Can there be any thing more ridiculous, than that a father should waste his own money, and his son's time, in setting him to learn the Roman language, when, at the same time, he designs him for a trade, wherein he, having no use of Latin, fails not to forget that little which he brought from school, and which it is ten to one he abhors for the ill usage it procured him? Could it be believed, unless we had every where amongst us examples of it, that a child should be forced to learn the rudiments of a language, which he is never to use in the course of life that he is designed to, and neglect all the while the writing a good hand, and casting accounts, which are of great advantage in all conditions of life, and to most trades indispensably necessary? But though these qualifications, requisite to trade and commerce, and the business of the world, are seldom or never to be had at grammar-schools; yet thither not only gentlemen send their younger sons intended for trades, but even tradesmen and farmers fail not to send their children, though they have neither intention nor ability to make them scholars. If you ask them, why they do this? they think it as strange a question, as if you should ask them why they go to church? Custom serves for reason, and has, to those that take it for reason, so consecrated this method, that it is almost religiously observed by them; and they stick to it, as if their children had scarce an orthodox education, unless they learned Lilly's grammar.[4]

§ 165. But how necessary soever Latin be to some, and is thought to be to others, to whom it is of no man-

[4] William Lily, or Lilye (ca. 1468–1522), intimate of Thomas More and Erasmus, a fine Greek and Latin scholar, appointed by Colet the first high master of St. Paul's School in 1510. His *Brevissima institutio*, corrected by Erasmus, became a famous Latin grammar that continued to be used in Locke's time and after.—P. G.

ner of use or service, yet the ordinary way of learning it in a grammar-school, is that, which having had thoughts about, I cannot be forward to encourage. The reasons against it are so evident and cogent, that they have prevailed with some intelligent persons to quit the ordinary road, not without success, though the method made use of was not exactly that which I imagine the easiest, and in short is this: to trouble the child with no grammar at all, but to have Latin, as English has been, without the perplexity of rules, talked into him; for, if you will consider it, Latin is no more unknown to a child, when he comes into the world, than English: and yet he learns English without master, rule, or grammar: and so might he Latin too, as Tully[5] did, if he had somebody always to talk to him in this language. And when we so often see a Frenchwoman teach an English girl to speak and read French perfectly, in a year or two, without any rule of grammar, or any thing else, but prattling to her; I cannot but wonder, how gentlemen have overseen this way for their sons, and thought them more dull or incapable than their daughters.

§ 166. If therefore a man could be got, who, himself speaking good Latin, would always be about your son, talk constantly to him, and suffer him to speak or read nothing else, this will be the true and genuine way, and that which I would propose, not only as the easiest and best, wherein a child might, without pains or chiding, get a language, which others are wont to be whipped for at school, six or seven years together; but also as that, wherein at the same time he might have his mind and manners formed, and he be instructed to boot in several

[5] Marcus Tullius Cicero (106–43 B.C.), familiarly called Tully by educated Englishmen through the eighteenth century, a mark of the high esteem in which Cicero was held.—P. G.

sciences, such as are a good part of geography, astronomy, chronology, anatomy, besides some parts of history, and all other parts of knowledge of things, that fall under the senses, and require little more than memory. For there, if we would take the true way, our knowledge should begin, and in those things be laid the foundation; and not in the abstract notions of logic and metaphysics, which are fitter to amuse, than inform the understanding, in its first setting out towards knowledge. When young men have had their heads employed a while in those abstract speculations, without finding the success and improvement, or that use of them which they expected, they are apt to have mean thoughts either of learning or themselves; they are tempted to quit their studies, and throw away their books, as containing nothing but hard words, and empty sounds; or else to conclude, that if there be any real knowledge in them, they themselves have not understandings capable of it. That this is so, perhaps I could assure you upon my own experience. Amongst other things to be learned by a young gentleman in this method, whilst others of his age are wholly taken up with Latin and languages, I may also set down geometry for one, having known a young gentleman, bred something after this way, able to demonstrate several propositions in Euclid, before he was thirteen.

§ 167. But if such a man cannot be got, who speaks good Latin, and, being able to instruct your son in all these parts of knowledge, will undertake it by this method; the next best is to have him taught as near this way as may be, which is by taking some easy and pleasant book, such as Æsop's Fables, and writing the English translation (made as literal as it can be) in one line, and the Latin words, which answer each of them, just over it in another. These let him read every day over and over again, till he perfectly understands the Latin; and then go on to another fable, till he be also perfect in that, not omitting what he is already perfect in, but sometimes reviewing that, to keep it in his memory. And when he comes to write, let these be set him for copies; which, with the exercise of his hand, will also advance him in Latin. This being a more imperfect way than by talking Latin unto him, the formation of the verbs first, and afterwards the declensions of the nouns and pronouns perfectly learnt by heart, may facilitate his acquaintance with the genius and manner of the Latin tongue, which varies the signification of verbs and nouns, not as the modern languages do, by particles prefixed, but by changing the last syllables. More than this of grammar I think he need not have, till he can read himself "Sanctii Minerva," with Scioppius and Perizonius's notes.[6]

In teaching of children this too, I think, it is to be observed, that in most cases, where they stick, they are not to be farther puzzled, by putting them upon finding it out themselves; as by asking such questions as these, viz. Which is the nominative case in the sentence they are to construe? or demanding what "aufero" signifies, to lead them to the knowledge what "abstulere" signifies, &c. when they cannot readily tell. This wastes time only in disturbing them; for whilst they are learning, and applying themselves with attention, they are to be kept in good humour, and every thing made easy to them, and as pleasant as possible. Therefore, wherever they are at a

---

[6] *Minerva, seu de causis linguae Latinae Commentarius* (1587), by Francesco Sanchez, called Sanctius (1523–1601). His popular textbook was later edited by Caspar Schoppe, called Scioppius (1576–1649), and Jacob Voorbroek, known as Perizonius (1651–1715). This "collaboration" illustrates the international character of scholarship in early modern Europe: Sanchez was a Spaniard, Scioppius a German, and Perizonius a Dutchman.—P. G.

stand, and are willing to go forwards, help them presently over the difficulty without any rebuke or chiding: remembering that, where harsher ways are taken, they are the effect only of pride and peevishness in the teacher, who expects children should instantly be masters of as much as he knows: whereas he should rather consider, that his business is to settle in them habits, not angrily to inculcate rules, which serve for little in the conduct of our lives; at least are of no use to children, who forget them as soon as given. In sciences where their reason is to be exercised, I will not deny, but this method may sometimes be varied, and difficulties proposed on purpose to excite industry, and accustom the mind to employ its whole strength and sagacity in reasoning. But yet, I guess, this is not to be done to children whilst very young; nor at their entrance upon any sort of knowledge: then every thing of itself is difficult, and the great use and skill of a teacher is to make all as easy as he can. But particularly in learning of languages there is least occasion for posing of children. For languages being to be learned by rote, custom, and memory, are then spoken in greatest perfection, when all rules of grammar are utterly forgotten. I grant the grammar of a language is sometimes very carefully to be studied: but it is only to be studied by a grown man, when he applies himself to the understanding of any language critically, which is seldom the business of any but professed scholars. This, I think, will be agreed to, that, if a gentleman be to study any language, it ought to be that of his own country, that he may understand the language, which he has constant use of, with the utmost accuracy.

There is yet a farther reason, why masters and teachers should raise no difficulties to their scholars; but, on the contrary, should smooth their way, and readily help them forwards, where they find them stop. Children's minds are narrow and weak, and usually susceptible but of one thought at once. Whatever is in a child's head, fills it for the time, especially if set on with any passion. It should therefore be the skill and art of the teacher, to clear their heads of all other thoughts, whilst they are learning of any thing, the better to make room for what he would instil into them, that it may be received with attention and application, without which it leaves no impression. The natural temper of children disposes their minds to wander. Novelty alone takes them; whatever that presents, they are presently eager to have a taste of, and are as soon satiated with it. They quickly grow weary of the same thing, and so have almost their whole delight in change and variety. It is a contradiction to the natural state of childhood, for them to fix their fleeting thoughts. Whether this be owing to the temper of their brains, or the quickness or instability of their animal spirits, over which the mind has not yet got a full command; this is visible, that it is a pain to children to keep their thoughts steady to any thing. A lasting continued attention is one of the hardest tasks can be imposed on them: and therefore, he that requires their application, should endeavour to make what he proposes as grateful and agreeable as possible; at least, he ought to take care not to join any displeasing or frightful idea with it. If they come not to their books with some kind of liking and relish, it is no wonder their thoughts should be perpetually shifting from what disgusts them, and seek better entertainment in more pleasing objects, after which they will unavoidably be gadding.

It is, I know, the usual method of tutors, to endeavour to procure attention in their scholars, and to fix their minds to the business in hand, by rebukes and corrections, if they find them ever so little wandering. But such treatment is sure to produce the quite contrary effect. Passionate words or blows from the tutor fill the child's mind with terror and affrightment, which immediately takes it wholly up, and leaves no room for other impressions. I believe there is nobody, that reads this, but may recollect, what disorder hasty or imperious words from his parents or teachers have caused in his thoughts; how for the time it has turned his brains, so that he scarce knew what was said by, or to him: he presently lost the sight of what he was upon; his mind was filled with disorder and confusion, and in that state was no longer capable of attention to any thing else.

It is true, parents and governors ought to settle and establish their authority, by an awe over the minds of those under their tuition; and to rule them by that: but when they have got an ascendant over them, they should use it with great moderation, and not make themselves such scarecrows, that their scholars should always tremble in their sight. Such an austerity may make their government easy to themselves, but of very little use to their pupils. It is impossible children should learn any thing, whilst their thoughts are possessed and disturbed with any passion, especially fear, which makes the strongest impression on their yet tender and weak spirits. Keep the mind in an easy calm temper, when you would have it receive your instructions, or any increase of knowledge. It is as impossible to draw fair and regular characters on a trembling mind, as on a shaking paper.

The great skill of a teacher is to get and keep the attention of his scholar: whilst he has that, he is sure to advance as fast as the learner's abilities will carry him; and without that, all his bustle and pother will be to little or no purpose. To attain this, he should make the child comprehend (as much as may be) the usefulness of what he teaches him; and let him see, by what he has learned, that he can do something which he could not do before; something which gives him some power and real advantage above others, who are ignorant of it. To this he should add sweetness in all his instructions; and by a certain tenderness in his whole carriage, make the child sensible that he loves him, and designs nothing but his good; the only way to beget love in the child, which will make him hearken to his lessons, and relish what he teaches him.

Nothing but obstinacy should meet with any imperiousness or rough usage. All other faults should be corrected with a gentle hand; and kind encouraging words will work better and more effectually upon a willing mind, and even prevent a good deal of that perverseness, which rough and imperious usage often produces in well-disposed and generous minds. It is true, obstinacy and wilful neglects must be mastered, even though it cost blows to do it: but I am apt to think perverseness in the pupils is often the effect of frowardness in the tutor; and that most children would seldom have deserved blows, if needless and misapplied roughness had not taught them ill-nature, and given them an aversion to their teacher, and all that comes from him.

Inadvertency, forgetfulness, unsteadiness, and wandering of thought, are the natural faults of childhood: and therefore, when they are not observed to be wilful, are to be mentioned softly, and gained upon by time. If every slip of this kind produces anger and rating, the occasions of rebuke and corrections will return so often, that the tutor will be a constant terror and uneasiness to his pupils; which one thing is enough to hinder their profiting by his lessons, and to defeat all his methods of instruction.

Let the awe he has got upon their minds be so tempered with the constant marks of tenderness and good
will, that affection may spur them to their duty, and make
them find a pleasure in complying with his dictates. This
will bring them with satisfaction to their tutor; make
them hearken to him, as to one who is their friend, that
cherishes them, and takes pains for their good; this will
keep their thoughts easy and free, whilst they are with
him, the only temper wherein the mind is capable of
receiving new informations, and of admitting into itself
those impressions, which if not taken and retained, all
that they and their teacher do together is lost labour;
there is much uneasiness, and little learning.

§ 168. When, by this way of interlining Latin and
English one with another, he has got a moderate knowledge of the Latin tongue, he may then be advanced a
little farther to the reading of some other easy Latin book,
such as Justin,[7] or Eutropius;[8] and to make the reading
and understanding of it the less tedious and difficult to
him, let him help himself, if he please, with the English
translation. Nor let the objection, that he will then know
it only by rote, fright any one. This, when well considered,
is not of any moment against, but plainly for, this way
of learning a language; for languages are only to be
learned by rote; and a man, who does not speak English
or Latin perfectly by rote, so that having thought of the
thing he would speak of, his tongue of course, without

[7] Junianus Justinus (probably second century A.D.). His *His-
toriarum Philippicarum libri XLIV*, as he himself admitted, was a
compilation of an earlier history of the world by Pompeius Trogus,
now lost. His anthology, widely used in the Middle Ages, owed
much of its popularity to the clarity of its style.—P. G.

[8] Eutropius (*fl.* second half of fourth century A.D.) compiled a history of Rome, *Breviarium historiae Romanae,* from its founding down
to his own time. Despite its lack of originality, the work was an
ideal textbook because of its simple Latin.—P. G.

thought of rule of grammar, falls into the proper expression and idiom of that language, does not speak it well, nor is master of it. And I would fain have any one name to me that tongue, that any one can learn or speak as he should do, by the rules of grammar. Languages were made not by rules or art, but by accident, and the common use of the people. And he that will speak them well, has no other rule but that; nor any thing to trust to but his memory, and the habit of speaking after the fashion learned from those that are allowed to speak properly, which, in other words, is only to speak by rote.

It will possibly be asked here, Is grammar then of no use? And have those who have taken so much pains in reducing several languages to rules and observations, who have writ so much about declensions and conjugations, about concords and syntaxis, lost their labour, and been learned to no purpose? I say not so; grammar has its place too. But this I think I may say, there is more stir a great deal made with it than there needs, and those are tormented about it, to whom it does not at all belong; I mean children, at the age wherein they are usually perplexed with it in grammar-schools.

There is nothing more evident, than that languages learned by rote serve well enough for the common affairs of life, and ordinary commerce. Nay, persons of quality of the softer sex, and such of them as have spent their time in well-bred company, show us, that this plain natural way, without the least study or knowledge of grammar, can carry them to a great degree of elegancy and politeness in their language: and there are ladies who, without knowing what tenses and participles, adverbs and prepositions are, speak as properly, and as correctly, (they might take it for an ill compliment, if I said as any country school-master) as most gentlemen who have been bred up in the ordinary methods of grammar-schools. Grammar, therefore, we see may be spared in some cases. The question then will be, To whom should it be taught, and when? To this I answer,

1. Men learn languages for the ordinary intercourse of society, and communication of thoughts in common life, without any farther design in their use of them. And for this purpose the original way of learning a language by conversation not only serves well enough, but is to be preferred, as the most expedite, proper, and natural. Therefore, to this use of language one may answer, that grammar is not necessary. This so many of my readers must be forced to allow, as understand what I here say, and who, conversing with others, understand them without having ever been taught the grammar of the English tongue: which I suppose is the case of incomparably the greatest part of Englishmen; of whom I have never yet known any one who learned his mother-tongue by rules.

2. Others there are, the greatest part of whose business in this world is to be done with their tongues, and with their pens; and to those it is convenient, if not necessary, that they should speak properly and correctly, whereby they may let their thoughts into other men's minds the more easily, and with the greater impression. Upon this account it is, that any sort of speaking, so as will make him be understood, is not thought enough for a gentleman. He ought to study grammar, amongst the other helps of speaking well; but it must be the grammar of his own tongue, of the language he uses, that he may understand his own country speech nicely, and speak it properly, without shocking the ears of those it is addressed to with solecisms and offensive irregularities. And to this purpose grammar is necessary; but it is the grammar only of their own proper tongues, and to those only who would take

pains in cultivating their language, and in perfecting their styles. Whether all gentlemen should not do this, I leave to be considered, since the want of propriety, and grammatical exactness, is thought very misbecoming one of that rank, and usually draws on one guilty of such faults the censure of having had a lower breeding, and worse company, than suits with his quality. If this be so, (as I suppose it is) it will be matter of wonder, why young gentlemen are forced to learn the grammars of foreign and dead languages, and are never once told of the grammar of their own tongues: they do not so much as know there is any such thing, much less is it made their business to be instructed in it. Nor is their own language ever proposed to them as worthy their care and cultivating, though they have daily use of it, and are not seldom in the future course of their lives judged of, by their handsome or awkward way of expressing themselves in it. Whereas the languages whose grammars they have been so much employed in, are such as probably they shall scarce ever speak or write; or, if upon occasion this should happen, they shall be excused for the mistakes and faults they make in it. Would not a Chinese, who took notice of this way of breeding, be apt to imagine, that all our young gentlemen were designed to be teachers and professors of the dead languages of foreign countries, and not to be men of business in their own?

3. There is a third sort of men, who apply themselves to two or three foreign, dead (and which amongst us are called the learned) languages, make them their study, and pique themselves upon their skill in them. No doubt those who propose to themselves the learning of any language with this view, and would be critically exact in it, ought carefully to study the grammar of it. I would not be mistaken here, as if this were to undervalue Greek and Latin:

I grant these are languages of great use and excellency; and a man can have no place amongst the learned, in this part of the world, who is a stranger to them. But the knowledge a gentleman would ordinarily draw for his use, out of the Roman and Greek writers, I think he may attain without studying the grammars of those tongues, and, by bare reading, may come to understand them sufficiently for all his purposes. How much farther he shall at any time be concerned to look into the grammar and critical niceties of either of these tongues, he himself will be able to determine, when he comes to propose to himself the study of any thing that shall require it. Which brings me to the other part of the inquiry, viz.

"When grammar should be taught?"

To which, upon the premised grounds, the answer is obvious, viz.

That, if grammar ought to be taught at any time, it must be to one that can speak the language already: how else can he be taught the grammar of it? This, at least, is evident from the practice of the wise and learned nations amongst the ancients. They made it a part of education to cultivate their own, not foreign tongues. The Greeks counted all other nations barbarous, and had a contempt for their languages. And, though the Greek learning grew in credit amongst the Romans, towards the end of their commonwealth, yet it was the Roman tongue that was made the study of their youth: their own language they were to make use of, and therefore it was their own language they were instructed and exercised in.

But more particularly to determine the proper season for grammar; I do not see how it can reasonably be made any one's study, but as an introduction to rhetoric: when it is thought time to put any one upon the care of polishing his tongue, and of speaking better than the illiterate, then is the time for him to be instructed in the rules of grammar, and not before. For grammar being to teach men not to speak, but to speak correctly, and according to the exact rules of the tongue, which is one part of elegancy, there is little use of the one to him that has no need of the other; where rhetoric is not necessary, grammar may be spared. I know not why any one should waste his time and beat his head about the Latin grammar, who does not intend to be a critic, or make speeches, and write despatches in it. When any one finds in himself a necessity or disposition to study any foreign language to the bottom, and to be nicely exact in the knowledge of it, it will be time enough to take a grammatical survey of it. If his use of it be only to understand some books writ in it without a critical knowledge of the tongue itself, reading alone, as I have said, will attain this end, without charging the mind with the multiplied rules and intricacies of grammar.

§ 169. For the exercise of his writing, let him sometimes translate Latin into English: but the learning of Latin being nothing but the learning of words, a very unpleasant business both to young and old, join as much other real knowledge with it as you can, beginning still with that which lies most obvious to the senses; such as is the knowledge of minerals, plants, and animals, and particularly timber and fruit trees, their parts and ways of propagation, wherein a great deal may be taught a child, which will not be useless to the man. But more especially geography, astronomy, and anatomy. But, whatever you are teaching him, have a care still, that you do not clog him with too much at once; or make any thing his business but downright virtue, or reprove him for any thing but vice, or some apparent tendency to it.

§ 170. But, if, after all, his fate be to go to school to

get the Latin tongue, it will be in vain to talk to you concerning the method I think best to be observed in schools.
You must submit to that you find there, not expect to
have it changed for your son; but yet by all means obtain, if you can, that he be not employed in making
Latin themes and declamations, and, least of all, verses of
any kind. You may insist on it, if it will do any good, that
you have no design to make him either a Latin orator or
poet, but barely would have him understand perfectly a
Latin author; and that you observe those who teach any
of the modern languages, and that with success, never
amuse their scholars to make speeches or verses either in
French or Italian, their business being language barely,
and not invention.

§ 171. But to tell you, a little more fully, why I would
not have him exercised in making of themes and verses:
1. As to themes, they have, I confess, the pretence of something useful, which is to teach people to speak handsomely
and well on any subject; which, if it could be attained
this way, I own, would be a great advantage; there being
nothing more becoming a gentleman, nor more useful in
all the occurrences of life, than to be able, on any occasion, to speak well, and to the purpose. But this I say,
that the making of themes, as is usual in schools, helps
not one jot towards it: for do but consider what it is in
making a theme that a young lad is employed about; it is
to make a speech on some Latin saying, as "Omnia vincit
amor," [9] or "Non licet in bello bis peccare," [10] &c. And
here the poor lad, who wants knowledge of those things
he is to speak of, which is to be had only from time and

[9] The full line from Vergil's *Eclogues* x. 69, reads: *"Omnia vincit
amor; et nos cedamus amori"* ("Love conquers all; and we should
yield to love").—P. G.

[10] "In war one is not allowed to blunder twice" (Latin proverb).—
P. G.

observation, must set his invention on the rack, to say
something where he knows nothing, which is a sort of
Ægyptian tyranny, to bid them make bricks who have not
yet any of the materials. And therefore it is usual, in such
cases, for the poor children to go to those of higher forms
with this petition, "Pray give me a little sense;" which
whether it be more reasonable or more ridiculous, is not
easy to determine. Before a man can be in any capacity to
speak on any subject, it is necessary he be acquainted
with it; or else it is as foolish to set him to discourse of it,
as to set a blind man to talk of colours, or a deaf man of
music. And would you not think him a little cracked
who would require another to make an argument on a
moot-point, who understands nothing of our laws? And
what, I pray, do school-boys understand concerning those
matters, which are used to be proposed to them in their
themes, as subjects to discourse on, to whet and exercise
their fancies?

§ 172. In the next place, consider the language that
their themes are made in: it is Latin, a language foreign
in their country, and long since dead every where; a language which your son, it is a thousand to one, shall never
have an occasion once to make a speech in as long as he
lives, after he comes to be a man; and a language, wherein
the manner of expressing one's self is so far different from
our's, that to be perfect in that, would very little improve
the purity and facility of his English style. Besides that,
there is now so little room or use for set speeches in our
own language in any part of our English business, that I
can see no pretence for this sort of exercise in our schools;
unless it can be supposed, that the making of set Latin
speeches should be the way to teach men to speak well in
English extempore. The way to that I should think rather
to be this: that there should be proposed to young gentle-

men rational and useful questions, suited to their age and capacities, and on subjects not wholly unknown to them, nor out of their way: such as these, when they are ripe for exercises of this nature, they should, extempore, or after a little meditation upon the spot, speak to, without penning of any thing. For I ask, if he will examine the effects of this way of learning to speak well, who speak best in any business, when occasion calls them to it upon any debate; either those who have accustomed themselves to compose and write down beforehand what they would say; or those, who thinking only of the matter, to understand that as well as they can, use themselves only to speak extempore? And he that shall judge by this, will be little apt to think, that the accustoming him to studied speeches, and set compositions, is the way to fit a young gentleman for business.

§ 173. But, perhaps, we shall be told, it is to improve and perfect them in the Latin tongue. It is true, that is their proper business at school; but the making of themes is not the way to it: that perplexes their brains, about invention of things to be said, not about the signification of words to be learnt; and, when they are making a theme, it is thoughts they search and sweat for, and not language. But the learning and mastery of a tongue, being uneasy and unpleasant enough in itself, should not be cumbered with any other difficulties, as is done in this way of proceeding. In fine, if boys' invention be to be quickened by such exercise, let them make themes in English, where they have facility, and a command of words, and will better see what kind of thoughts they have, when put into their own language: and, if the Latin tongue be to be learned, let it be done in the easiest way, without toiling and disgusting the mind by so uneasy an employment as that of making speeches joined to it.

§ 174. If these may be any reasons against children's making Latin themes at school, I have much more to say, and of more weight, against their making verses of any sort: for, if he has no genius to poetry, it is the most unreasonable thing in the world to torment a child, and waste his time about that which can never succeed; and, if he have a poetic vein, it is to me the strangest thing in the world, that the father should desire or suffer it to be cherished or improved. Methinks the parents should labour to have it stifled and suppressed as much as may be; and I know not what reason a father can have to wish his son a poet, who does not desire to have him bid defiance to all other callings and business: which is not yet the worst of the case; for if he proves a successful rhymer, and gets once the reputation of a wit, I desire it may be considered what company and places he is likely to spend his time in, nay, and estate too: for it is very seldom seen, that any one discovers mines of gold or silver in Parnassus. It is a pleasant air, but a barren soil; and there are very few instances of those who have added to their patrimony by any thing they have reaped from thence. Poetry and gaming, which usually go together, are alike in this too, that they seldom bring any advantage, but to those who have nothing else to live on. Men of estates almost constantly go away losers; and it is well if they escape at a cheaper rate than their whole estates, or the greatest part of them. If, therefore, you would not have your son the fiddle to every jovial company, without whom the sparks could not relish their wine, nor know how to pass an afternoon idly; if you would not have him waste his time and estate to divert others, and contemn the dirty acres left him by his ancestors, I do not think you will much care he should be a poet, or that his school-master should enter him in versifying. But yet, if any one will think poetry a desirable quality in his son, and that the study of it would raise his fancy and parts, he must needs yet confess, that, to that end, reading the excellent Greek and Roman poets is of more use than making bad verses of his own, in a language that is not his own. And he, whose design it is to excel in English poetry, would not, I guess, think the way to it were to make his first essays in Latin verses.

§ 175. Another thing, very ordinary in the vulgar method of grammar-schools, there is, of which I see no use at all, unless it be to balk young lads in the way to learning languages, which, in my opinion, should be made as easy and pleasant as may be; and that which was painful in it, as much as possible, quite removed. That which I mean, and here complain of, is, their being forced to learn by heart great parcels of the authors which are taught them; wherein I can discover no advantage at all, especially to the business they are upon. Languages are to be learnt only by reading and talking, and not by scraps of authors got by heart; which when a man's head is stuffed with, he has got the just furniture of a pedant, and it is the ready way to make him one, than which there is nothing less becoming a gentleman. For what can be more ridiculous, than to mix the rich and handsome thoughts and sayings of others with a deal of poor stuff of his own; which is thereby the more exposed; and has no other grace in it, nor will otherwise recommend the speaker, than a thread-bare russet coat would, that was set off with large patches of scarlet and glittering brocade? Indeed, where a passage comes in the way, whose matter is worth remembrance, and the expression of it very close and excellent (as there are many such in the ancient authors), it may not be amiss to lodge it in the minds of young scholars, and with such admirable strokes of those great masters sometimes exercise the memories of school-boys:

but their learning of their lessons by heart, as they happen to fall out in their books, without choice or distinction, I know not what it serves for, but to mispend their time and pains, and give them a disgust and aversion to their books, wherein they find nothing but useless trouble.

§ 176. I hear it is said, that children should be employed in getting things by heart, to exercise and improve their memories. I could wish this were said with as much authority of reason, as it is with forwardness of assurance; and that this practice were established upon good observation, more than old custom; for it is evident, that strength of memory is owing to a happy constitution, and not to any habitual improvement got by exercise. It is true, what the mind is intent upon, and for fear of letting it slip, often imprints afresh on itself by frequent reflection, that it is apt to retain, but still according to its own natural strength of retention. An impression made on bees-wax or lead will not last so long as on brass or steel. Indeed, if it be renewed often, it may last the longer; but every new reflecting on it is a new impression, and it is from thence one is to reckon, if one would know how long the mind retains it. But the learning pages of Latin by heart, no more fits the memory for retention of any thing else, than the graving of one sentence in lead, makes it the more capable of retaining firmly any other characters. If such a sort of exercise of the memory were able to give it strength, and improve our parts, players of all other people must needs have the best memories, and be the best company: but whether the scraps they have got into their head this way, make them remember other things the better; and whether their parts be improved proportionably to the pains they have taken in getting by heart other sayings; experience will show. Memory is so necessary to all parts and conditions of life, and so little is to be done without it, that we are not to fear it should grow dull and useless for want of exercise, if exercise would make it grow stronger. But I fear this faculty of the mind is not capable of much help and amendment in general, by any exercise or endeavour of ours, at least not by that used upon this pretence in grammar-schools. And if Xerxes was able to call every common soldier by his name, in his army, that consisted of no less than a hundred thousand men, I think it may be guessed, he got not this wonderful ability by learning his lessons by heart, when he was a boy. This method of exercising and improving the memory by toilsome repetitions, without book, of what they read, is, I think, little used in the education of princes; which, if it had that advantage talked of, should be as little neglected in them, as in the meanest school-boys: princes having as much need of good memories as any men living, and have generally an equal share in this faculty with other men: though it has never been taken care of this way. What the mind is intent upon, and careful of, that it remembers best, and for the reason above-mentioned: to which if method and order be joined, all is done, I think, that can be, for the help of a weak memory; and he that will take any other way to do it, especially that of charging it with a train of other people's words, which he that learns cares not for; will, I guess, scarce find the profit answer half the time and pains employed in it.

I do not mean hereby, that there should be no exercise given to children's memories. I think their memories should be employed, but not in learning by rote whole pages out of books, which, the lesson being once said, and that task over, are delivered up again to oblivion, and neglected for ever. This mends neither the memory nor the mind. What they should learn by heart out of authors, I have above-mentioned: and such wise and useful sentences being once given in charge to their memories, they should never be suffered to forget again, but be often called to account for them: whereby, besides the use those sayings may be to them in their future life, as so many good rules and observations; they will be taught to reflect often, and bethink themselves what they have to remember, which is the only way to make the memory quick and useful. The custom of frequent reflection will keep their minds from running adrift, and call their thoughts home from useless, inattentive roving: and therefore, I think, it may do well to give them something every day to remember; but something still, that is in itself worth the remembering, and what you would never have out of mind, whenever you call, or they themselves search for it. This will oblige them often to turn their thoughts inwards, than which you cannot wish them a better intellectual habit.

§ 177. But under whose care soever a child is put to be taught, during the tender and flexible years of his life, this is certain, it should be one who thinks Latin and language the least part of education; one, who knowing how much virtue, and a well-tempered soul, is to be preferred to any sort of learning or language, makes it his chief business to form the mind of his scholars, and give that a right disposition: which, if once got, though all the rest should be neglected, would, in due time, produce all the rest; and which if it be not got, and settled, so as to keep out ill and vicious habits, languages and sciences, and all the other accomplishments of education, will be to no purpose, but to make the worse or more dangerous man. And indeed, whatever stir there is made about getting of Latin, as the great and difficult business; his mother may teach it him herself, if she will but spend two or three hours in a day with him, and make him read the evan-

gelists in Latin to her: for she need but buy a Latin Testament, and having got somebody to mark the last syllable
but one, where it is long, in words above two syllables,
(which is enough to regulate her pronunciation, and ac-
centing the words) read daily in the Gospels; and then let
her avoid understanding them in Latin, if she can. And
when she understands the Evangelists in Latin, let her,
in the same manner, read Æsop's Fables, and so proceed
on to Eutropius, Justin, and other such books. I do not
mention this as an imagination of what I fancy may do,
but as of a thing I have known done, and the Latin
tongue, with ease, got this way.

But to return to what I was saying: he that takes on
him the charge of bringing up young men, especially
young gentlemen, should have something more in him
than Latin, more than even a knowledge in the liberal
sciences; he should be a person of eminent virtue and
prudence, and with good sense have good humour, and
the skill to carry himself with gravity, ease, and kindness,
in a constant conversation with his pupils. But of this I
have spoken at large in another place.

§ 178.   At the same time that he is learning French
and Latin, a child, as has been said, may also be entered
in arithmetic, geography, chronology, history, and geometry too. For if these be taught him in French or Latin,
when he begins once to understand either of these
tongues, he will get a knowledge in these sciences, and
the language to boot.

Geography, I think, should be begun with; for the
learning of the figure of the globe, the situation and
boundaries of the four parts of the world, and that of
particular kingdoms and countries, being only an exercise
of the eyes and memory, a child with pleasure will learn
and retain them: and this is so certain, that I now live in

the house with a child,[11] whom his mother has so well instructed this way in geography, that he knew the limits of the four parts of the world, could readily point, being asked, to any country upon the globe, or any county in the map of England; knew all the great rivers, promontories, straits, and bays in the world, and could find the longitude and latitude of any place, before he was six years old. These things, that he will thus learn by sight, and have by rote in his memory, are not all, I confess, that he is to learn upon the globes. But yet it is a good step and preparation to it, and will make the remainder much easier, when his judgment is grown ripe enough for it: besides that, it gets so much time now, and by the pleasure of knowing things, leads him on insensibly to the gaining of languages.

§ 179. When he has the natural parts of the globe well fixed in his memory, it may then be time to begin arithmetic. By the natural parts of the globe, I mean several positions of the parts of the earth and sea, under different names and distinctions of countries; not coming yet to those artificial and imaginary lines, which have been invented, and are only supposed, for the better improvement of that science.

§ 180. Arithmetic is the easiest, and, consequently, the first sort of abstract reasoning, which the mind commonly bears, or accustoms itself to: and is of so general use in all parts of life and business, that scarce any thing is to be done without it. This is certain, a man cannot have too much of it, nor too perfectly; he should therefore begin to be exercised in counting, as soon, and as far,

[11] The child referred to here is Francis Cudworth Masham, born in 1686, son of Sir Francis Masham, with whom Locke made his home from 1691 until his death in 1704. It appears that the boy was brought up according to Locke's principles, largely at the insistence of Francis' remarkable mother.—P. G.

as he is capable of it; and do something in it every day, till he is master of the art of numbers. When he understands addition and subtraction, he may then be advanced farther in geography, and after he is acquainted with the poles, zones, parallel circles, and meridians, be taught longitude and latitude, and by them be made to understand the use of maps, and by the numbers placed on their sides, to know the respective situation of countries, and how to find them out on the terrestrial globe. Which when he can readily do, he may then be entered in the celestial; and there going over all the circles again, with a more particular observation of the ecliptic or zodiac, to fix them all very clearly and distinctly in his mind, he may be taught the figure and position of the several constellations, which may be showed him first upon the globe, and then in the heavens.

When that is done, and he knows pretty well the constellations of this our hemisphere, it may be time to give him some notions of this our planetary world, and to that purpose it may not be amiss to make him a draught of the Copernican system; and therein explain to him the situation of the planets, their respective distances from the sun, the centre of their revolutions. This will prepare him to understand the motion and theory of the planets, the most easy and natural way. For, since astronomers no longer doubt of the motion of the planets about the sun, it is fit he should proceed upon that hypothesis, which is not only the simplest and least perplexed for a learner, but also the likeliest to be true in itself. But in this, as in all other parts of instruction, great care must be taken with children, to begin with that which is plain and simple, and to teach them as little as can be at once, and settle that well in their heads, before you proceed to the next, or any thing new in that science. Give them first one simple idea, and see that they take it right, and perfectly comprehend it, before you go any farther; and then add some other simple idea, which lies next in your way to what you aim at; and so proceeding by gentle and insensible steps, children, without confusion and amazement, will have their understandings opened, and their thoughts extended, farther than could have been expected. And when any one has learned any thing himself, there is no such way to fix it in his memory, and to encourage him to go on, as to set him to teach it others.

§ 181.   When he has once got such an acquaintance with the globes, as is above-mentioned, he may be fit to be tried a little in geometry; wherein I think the six first books of Euclid enough for him to be taught. For I am in some doubt, whether more to a man of business be necessary or useful; at least if he have a genius and inclination to it, being entered so far by his tutor, he will be able to go on of himself without a teacher.

The globes, therefore, must be studied, and that diligently, and, I think, may be begun betimes, if the tutor will but be careful to distinguish what the child is capable of knowing, and what not; for which this may be a rule, that perhaps will go a pretty way, (viz.) that children may be taught any thing that falls under their senses, especially their sight, as far as their memories only are exercised: and thus a child very young may learn, which is the equator, which the meridian, &c. which Europe, and which England, upon the globes, as soon almost as he knows the rooms of the house he lives in; if care be taken not to teach him too much at once, nor to set him upon a new part, till that, which he is upon, be perfectly learned and fixed in his memory.

§ 182.   With geography, chronology ought to go hand

in hand; I mean the general part of it, so that he may have in his mind a view of the whole current of time, and the several considerable epochs that are made use of in history. Without these two, history, which is the great mistress of prudence and civil knowledge; and ought to be the proper study of a gentleman, or man of business in the world; without geography and chronology, I say, history will be very ill retained, and very little useful; but be only a jumble of matters of fact, confusedly heaped together without order or instruction. It is by these two that the actions of mankind are ranked into their proper places of times and countries; under which circumstances, they are not only much easier kept in the memory, but, in that natural order, are only capable to afford those observations, which make a man the better and the abler for reading them.

§ 183. When I speak of chronology as a science he should be perfect in, I do not mean the little controversies that are in it. These are endless, and most of them of so little importance to a gentleman, as not to deserve to be inquired into, were they capable of an easy decision. And therefore all that learned noise and dust of the chronologist is wholly to be avoided. The most useful book I have seen in that part of learning, is a small treatise of Strauchius, which is printed in twelves, under the title of "Breviarium Chronologicum," [12] out of which may be selected all that is necessary to be taught a young gentleman concerning chronology; for all that is in that treatise a learner need not be cumbered with. He has in him the most remarkable or usual epochs reduced all to that of

[12] Aegidius Strauch, called Strauchius (1632–1682), Lutheran theologian, professor of history and mathematics at the University of Wittenberg. His *Breviarium chronologiae* (1657) was a popular chronology, widely reprinted and translated.—P. G.

the Julian period, which is the easiest, and plainest, and surest method, that can be made use of in chronology. To this treatise of Strauchius, Helvicus's tables[13] may be added, as a book to be turned to on all occasions.

§ 184. As nothing teaches, so nothing delights, more than history. The first of these recommends it to the study of grown men; the latter makes me think it the fittest for a young lad, who, as soon as he is instructed in chronology, and acquainted with the several epochs in use in this part of the world, and can reduce them to the Julian period, should then have some Latin history put into his hand. The choice should be directed by the easiness of the style; for wherever he begins, chronology will keep it from confusion; and the pleasantness of the subject inviting him to read, the language will insensibly be got, without that terrible vexation and uneasiness, which children suffer where they are put into books beyond their capacity, such as are the Roman orators and poets, only to learn the Roman language. When he has by reading mastered the easier, such perhaps as Justin, Eutropius, Quintus Curtius,[14] &c. the next degree to these will give him no great trouble: and thus, by a gradual progress from the plainest and easiest historians, he may at last come to read the most difficult and sublime of the Latin authors, such as are Tully, Virgil, and Horace.

§ 185. The knowledge of virtue, all along from the beginning, in all the instances he is capable of, being

[13] Christoph Helwig, called Helvicus (1581–1617), gifted educational reformer, professor of Hebrew, Greek, and theology at the University of Giessen. He wrote several chronologies, including *Theatrum historicum sive chronologiae systema novum* (1609) and *Synopsis historiae universalis* (1612), made especially useful by their tables.—P. G.

[14] Quintus Curtius (*fl.* probably first half of first century A.D.). His *De rebus gestis Alexandri magni* is an uncritical but well-written compilation. For the others, see notes 7 and 8.—P. G.

taught him, more by practice than rules; and the love of reputation, instead of satisfying his appetite, being made habitual in him; I know not whether he should read any other discourses of morality, but what he finds in the Bible; or have any system of ethics put into his hand, till he can read Tully's Offices,[15] not as a school-boy to learn Latin, but as one that would be informed in the principles and precepts of virtue, for the conduct of his life.

§ 186.   When he has pretty well digested Tully's Offices, and added to it "Puffendorf de Officio Hominis et Civis," [16] it may be seasonable to set him upon "Grotius de Jure Belli et Pacis," [17] or, which perhaps is the better of the two, "Puffendorf de Jure Naturali et Gentium," [18] wherein he will be instructed in the natural rights of men, and the original and foundations of society, and the duties resulting from thence. This general part of civil law and history are studies which a gentleman should not barely touch at, but constantly dwell upon, and never have done with. A virtuous and well-behaved young man, that is well versed in the general part of the civil law, (which concerns not the chicane of private cases, but the affairs and intercourse of civilized nations in general, grounded upon principles of reason) understands Latin

15 In Locke's time, as in the eighteenth-century Enlightenment, Cicero's *De officiis* was widely regarded as one of the unsurpassed masterpieces of antiquity on moral duties.—P. G.

16 Samuel Pufendorf (1632–1694), distinguished German jurist and historian. His *De officio hominis et civis* (1675) is an abridgment of his major work on natural and international law, *De jure naturae et gentium, libri octo* (1672), which carries on in the tradition of Grotius (see note 17).—P. G.

17 Huig van Groot, called Hugo Grotius (1583–1645), great international lawyer, originator of modern international law, Dutch statesman and theologian noted for his attempt to base the law of nations on the law of nature. His *De jure belli ac pacis* (1625) is his masterpiece.—P. G.

18 See note 16.—P. G.

well, and can write a good hand, one may turn loose into the world, with great assurance that he will find employment and esteem every where.

§ 187. It would be strange to suppose an English gentleman should be ignorant of the law of his country. This, whatever station he is in, is so requisite, that, from a justice of the peace to a minister of state, I know no place he can well fill without it. I do not mean the chicane or wrangling and captious part of the law; a gentleman whose business is to seek the true measures of right and wrong, and not the arts how to avoid doing the one, and secure himself in doing the other, ought to be as far from such a study of the law, as he is concerned diligently to apply himself to that wherein he may be serviceable to his country. And to that purpose I think the right way for a gentleman to study our law, which he does not design for his calling, is to take a view of our English constitution and government, in the ancient books of the common law, and some more modern writers, who out of them have given an account of this government. And having got a true idea of that, then to read our history, and with it join in every king's reign the laws then made. This will give an insight into the reason of our statutes, and show the true ground upon which they came to be made, and what weight they ought to have.

§ 188. Rhetoric and logic being the arts that in the ordinary method usually follow immediately after grammar, it may perhaps be wondered, that I have said so little of them. The reason is, because of the little advantage young people receive by them; for I have seldom or never observed any one to get the skill of reasoning well, or speaking handsomely, by studying those rules which pretend to teach it: and therefore I would have a young gentleman take a view of them in the shortest systems could be found, without dwelling long on the contemplation and study of those formalities. Right reasoning is founded on something else than the predicaments and predicables, and does not consist in talking in mode and figure itself. But it is besides my present business to enlarge upon this speculation. To come therefore to what we have in hand; if you would have your son reason well, let him read Chillingworth;[19] and if you would have him speak well, let him be conversant in Tully, to give him the true idea of eloquence; and let him read those things that are well writ in English, to perfect his style in the purity of our language.

§ 189. If the use and end of right reasoning be to have right notions, and a right judgment of things; to distinguish betwixt truth and falsehood, right and wrong, and to act accordingly; be sure not to let your son be bred up in the art and formality of disputing, either practising it himself, or admiring it in others; unless, instead of an able man, you desire to have him an insignificant wrangler, opiniatre in discourse, and priding himself in contradicting others; or, which is worse, questioning every thing, and thinking there is no such thing as truth to be sought, but only victory, in disputing. There cannot be any thing so disingenuous, so misbecoming a gentleman, or any one who pretends to be a rational creature, as not to yield to plain reason, and the conviction of clear arguments. For this, in short, is the way and perfection of logical disputes, that the opponent never

[19] William Chillingworth (1602–1644), English theologian who was converted to Roman Catholicism but returned to the Church of England and took holy orders in it in 1638. In the same year, he published *The Religion of Protestants a Safe Way to Salvation,* in which he assailed his former coreligionists and defended the Protestant position that the Scriptures are adequate authority in religious affairs.—P. G.

takes any answer, nor the respondent ever yields to any argument. This neither of them must do, whatever becomes of truth or knowledge, unless he will pass for a poor baffled wretch, and lie under the disgrace of not being able to maintain whatever he has once affirmed, which is the great aim and glory in disputing. Truth is to be found and supported by a mature and due consideration of things themselves, and not by artificial terms and ways of arguing: these lead not men so much into the discovery of truth, as into a captious and fallacious use of doubtful words, which is the most useless and most offensive way of talking, and such as least suits a gentleman or a lover of truth of any thing in the world.

There can scarce be a greater defect in a gentleman, than not to express himself well, either in writing or speaking. But yet, I think, I may ask my reader, Whether he doth not know a great many, who live upon their estates, and so, with the name, should have the qualities of gentlemen, who cannot so much as tell a story as they should, much less speak clearly and persuasively in any business? This I think not to be so much their fault, as the fault of their education; for I must, without partiality, do my countrymen this right, that where they apply themselves, I see none of their neighbours outgo them. They have been taught rhetoric, but yet never taught how to express themselves handsomely with their tongues, or pens, in the language they are always to use; as if the names of the figures, that embellished the discourses of those who understood the art of speaking, were the very art and skill of speaking well. This, as all other things of practice, is to be learned not by a few or a great many rules given, but by exercise and application, according to good rules, or rather patterns, till habits are got, and a facility of doing it well.

Agreeable hereunto, perhaps it might not be amiss to make children, as soon as they are capable of it, often to tell a story of any thing they know; and to correct at first the most remarkable fault they are guilty of, in their way of putting it together. When that fault is cured, then to show them the next, and so on, till, one after another, all, at least the gross ones, are mended. When they can tell tales pretty well, then it may be time to make them write them. The Fables of Æsop, the only book almost that I know fit for children, may afford them matter for this exercise of writing English, as well as for reading and translating, to enter them in the Latin tongue. When they are got past the faults of grammar, and can join in a continued coherent discourse the several parts of a story, without bald and unhandsome forms of transition (as is usual) often repeated; he that desires to perfect them yet farther in this, which is the first step to speaking well, and needs no invention, may have recourse to Tully; and by putting in practice those rules, which that master of eloquence gives in his first book "De Inventione," § 20. make them know wherein the skill and graces of an handsome narrative, according to the several subjects and designs of it, lie. Of each of which rules fit examples may be found out, and therein they may be shown how others have practised them. The ancient classic authors afford plenty of such examples, which they should be made not only to translate, but have set before them as patterns for their daily imitation.

When they understand how to write English with due connexion, propriety, and order, and are pretty well masters of a tolerable narrative style, they may be advanced to writing of letters; wherein they should not be put upon any strains of wit or compliment, but taught to express their own plain easy sense, without any incoherence, confusion, or roughness. And when they are perfect in this, they may, to raise their thoughts, have set before them the example of Voiture's,[20] for the entertainment of their friends at a distance, with letters of compliment, mirth, raillery, or diversion; and Tully's epistles, as the best pattern, whether for business or conversation. The writing of letters has so much to do in all the occurrences of human life, that no gentleman can avoid showing himself in this kind of writing: occasions will daily force him to make this use of his pen, which, besides the consequences, that, in his affairs, his well or ill managing of it often draws after it, always lays him open to a severer examination of his breeding, sense, and abilities, than oral discourses; whose transient faults, dying for the most part with the sound that gives them life, and so not subject to a strict review, more easily escape observation and censure.

Had the methods of education been directed to their right end, one would have thought this, so necessary a part, could not have been neglected, whilst themes and verses in Latin, of no use at all, were so constantly every where pressed, to the racking of children's inventions beyond their strength, and hindering their cheerful progress in learning the tongues, by unnatural difficulties. But custom has so ordained it, and who dares disobey? And would it not be very unreasonable to require of a learned country schoolmaster (who has all the tropes and figures in Farnaby's rhetoric[21] at his fingers' ends), to teach his scholar to express himself handsomely in English, when it appears to be so little his business or thought, that the

[20] Vincent Voiture (1597–1648), French poet and man of letters. While his literary work was an example of preciosity, it had wide popularity.—P. G.

[21] Thomas Farnaby (1575?–1647), classical scholar and adventurous traveler who accompanied Drake and Hawkins on their voyages but

boy's mother (despised, it is like, as illiterate, for not
having read a system of logic and rhetoric), outdoes him
in it?

To write and speak correctly gives a grace, and gains
a favourable attention to what one has to say: and, since
it is English that an English gentleman will have constant
use of, that is the language he should chiefly cultivate, and
wherein most care should be taken to polish and perfect
his style. To speak or write better Latin than English may
make a man be talked of; but he would find it more to his
purpose to express himself well in his own tongue, that
he uses every moment, than to have the vain commendation of others for a very insignificant quality. This I find
universally neglected, and no care taken any where to improve young men in their own language, that they may
thoroughly understand and be masters of it. If any one
among us have a facility or purity more than ordinary in
his mother-tongue, it is owing to chance, or his genius, or
any thing, rather than to his education, or any care of his
teacher. To mind what English his pupil speaks or writes,
is below the dignity of one bred up amongst Greek and
Latin, though he have but little of them himself. These
are the learned languages, fit only for learned men to
meddle with and teach; English is the language of the
illiterate vulgar; though yet we see the policy of some of
our neighbours hath not thought it beneath the public
care to promote and reward the improvement of their
own language. Polishing and enriching their tongue is no
small business amongst them; it hath colleges and stipends
appointed it, and there is raised amongst them a great
ambition and emulation of writing correctly: and we see

---

then settled down, edited classical texts with conspicuous success,
and gained a European reputation with a private school he conducted in London. In 1625, he published a textbook, *Index
Rhetoricus,* which went into many editions.—P. G.

what they are come to by it, and how far they have spread one of the worst languages, possibly, in this part of the world, if we look upon it as it was in some few reigns backwards, whatever it be now. The great men amongst the Romans were daily exercising themselves in their own language; and we find yet upon record the names of orators, who taught some of their emperors Latin, though it were their mother tongue.

It is plain the Greeks were yet more nice in theirs; all other speech was barbarous to them but their own, and no foreign language appears to have been studied or valued amongst that learned and acute people; though it be past doubt, that they borrowed their learning and philosophy from abroad.

I am not here speaking against Greek and Latin; I think they ought to be studied, and the Latin at least, understood well, by every gentleman. But whatever foreign languages a young man meddles with (and the more he knows, the better), that which he should critically study, and labour to get a facility, clearness, and elegancy to express himself in, should be his own, and to this purpose he should daily be exercised in it.

§ 190. Natural philosophy, as a speculative science, I imagine, we have none; and perhaps I may think I have reason to say, we never shall be able to make a science of it. The works of nature are contrived by a wisdom, and operate by ways, too far surpassing our faculties to discover, or capacities to conceive, for us ever to be able to reduce them into a science. Natural philosophy being the knowledge of the principles, properties, and operations of things, as they are in themselves, I imagine there are two parts of it, one comprehending spirits, with their nature and qualities; and the other bodies. The first of these is usually referred to metaphysics: but under what title

soever the consideration of spirits comes, I think it ought
to go before the study of matter and body, not as a science
that can be methodized into a system, and treated of, upon
principles of knowledge; but as an enlargement of our
minds towards a truer and fuller comprehension of the
intellectual world, to which we are led both by reason
and revelation. And since the clearest and largest discoveries we have of other spirits, besides God and our own
souls, is imparted to us from heaven by revelation, I think
the information, that at least young people should have of
them, should be taken from that revelation. To this purpose, I conclude, it would be well, if there were made a
good history of the Bible for young people to read;
wherein if every thing that is fit to be put into it were
laid down in its due order of time, and several things
omitted, which are suited only to riper age; that confusion, which is usually produced by promiscuous reading
of the Scripture, as it lies now bound up in our Bibles,
would be avoided; and also this other good obtained,
that by reading of it constantly, there would be instilled
into the minds of children a notion and belief of spirits,
they having so much to do, in all the transactions of that
history, which will be a good preparation to the study of
bodies. For, without the notion and allowance of spirit,
our philosophy will be lame and defective in one main
part of it, when it leaves out the contemplation of the
most excellent and powerful part of the creation.

§ 191. Of this history of the Bible, I think too it
would be well, if there were a short and plain epitome
made, containing the chief and most material heads for
children to be conversant in, as soon as they can read.
This, though it will lead them early into some notion of
spirits, yet is not contrary to what I said above, that I
would not have children troubled, whilst young, with

notions of spirits; whereby my meaning was, that I think it inconvenient, that their yet tender minds should receive early impressions of goblins, spectres, and apparitions, wherewith their maids, and those about them, are apt to fright them into a compliance of their orders, which often proves a great inconvenience to them all their lives after, by subjecting their minds to frights, fearful apprehensions, weakness, and superstition; which, when coming abroad into the world and conversation, they grow weary and ashamed of; it not seldom happens, that to make, as they think, a thorough cure, and ease themselves of a load, which has sat so heavy on them, they throw away the thoughts of all spirits together, and so run into the other, but worse extreme.

§ 192. The reason why I would have this premised to the study of bodies, and the doctrine of the Scriptures well imbibed, before young men be entered in natural philosophy, is, because matter being a thing that all our senses are constantly conversant with, it is so apt to possess the mind, and exclude all other beings but matter, that prejudice, grounded on such principles, often leaves no room for the admittance of spirits, or the allowing any such things as immaterial beings, "in rerum naturâ;" when yet it is evident, that by mere matter and motion, none of the great phænomena of nature can be resolved: to instance but in that common one of gravity, which I think impossible to be explained by any natural operation of matter, or any other law of motion, but the positive will of a superior Being so ordering it. And therefore since the deluge cannot be well explained, without admitting something out of the ordinary course of nature, I propose it to be considered, whether God's altering the centre of gravity in the earth for a time, (a thing as intelligible as gravity itself, which perhaps a little variation of causes, unknown to us, would produce), will not more easily account for Noah's flood, than any hypothesis yet made use of, to solve it.[22] I hear the great objection to this is, that it would produce but a partial deluge. But the alteration of the centre of gravity once allowed, it is no hard matter to conceive, that the divine power might make the centre of gravity, placed at a due distance from the centre of the earth, move round it in a convenient space of time; whereby the flood would become universal, and, as I think, answer all the phænomena of the deluge, as delivered by Moses, at an easier rate than those many hard suppositions that are made use of to explain it. But this is not a place for that argument, which is here only mentioned by the by, to show the necessity of having recourse to something beyond bare matter and its motion, in the explication of nature; to which the notions of spirits, and their power, as delivered in the Bible, where so much is attributed to their operation, may be a fit preparative; reserving to a fitter opportunity a fuller explication of this hypothesis, and the application of it to all the parts of the deluge, and any difficulties that can be supposed in the history of the flood, as recorded in the Scripture.

§ 193. But to return to the study of natural philosophy: though the world be full of systems of it, yet I cannot say, I know any one which can be taught a young man as a science, wherein he may be sure to find truth and certainty, which is what all sciences give an expectation of. I do not hence conclude, that none of them are to be read; it is necessary for a gentleman in this learned age to look into some of them, to fit himself for conversation:

[22] As J. W. Adamson notes in his edition of Locke's *Thoughts*, this is doubtless an allusion to ideas advanced by Thomas Burnet (*ca.* 1635–1715) in his *Sacred Theory of the Earth* (1684), an English version of an earlier Latin treatise of 1681.—P. G.

but whether that of Des Cartes be put into his hands, as that which is the most in fashion, or it be thought fit to give him a short view of that and several others also; I think the systems of natural philosophy that have obtained in this part of the world, are to be read more to know the hypotheses, and to understand the terms and ways of talking of the several sects, than with hopes to gain thereby a comprehensive scientifical and satisfactory knowledge of the works of nature: only this may be said, that the modern corpuscularians talk, in most things, more intelligibly than the peripatetics, who possessed the schools immediately before them. He that would look farther back, and acquaint himself with the several opinions of the ancients, may consult Dr. Cudworth's Intellectual System;[23] wherein that very learned author hath, with such accurateness and judgment, collected and explained the opinions of the Greek philosophers, that what principles they built on, and what were the chief hypotheses that divided them, is better to be seen in him than any where else that I know. But I would not deter any one from the study of nature, because all the knowledge we have, or possibly can have of it, cannot be brought into a science. There are very many things in it, that are convenient and necessary to be known to a gentleman; and a great many other, that will abundantly reward the pains of the curious with delight and advantage. But these, I think, are rather to be found amongst such writers, as have employed themselves in making rational experiments and observations, than in starting barely speculative systems. Such writings, there-

[23] Ralph Cudworth (1617–1688), English theologian who belonged to the philosophical group known as the Cambridge Platonists. His *True Intellectual System of the Universe* (1678) was published in part as a reply to Hobbesian materialism.—P. G.

fore, as many of Mr. Boyle's are, with others that have
writ of husbandry, planting, gardening, and the like, may
be fit for a gentleman, when he has a little acquainted
himself with some of the systems of natural philosophy
in fashion.

§ 194. Though the systems of physics that I have
met with afford little encouragement to look for certainty, or science, in any treatise, which shall pretend to
give us a body of natural philosophy from the first principles of bodies in general; yet the incomparable Mr. Newton has shown, how far mathematics, applied to some
parts of nature, may, upon principles that matter of fact
justify, carry us in the knowledge of some, as I may so
call them, particular provinces of the incomprehensible
universe. And if others could give us so good and clear
an account of other parts of nature, as he has of this our
planetary world, and the most considerable phænomena
observable in it, in his admirable book "Philosophiæ
naturalis Principia mathematica," [24] we might in time
hope to be furnished with more true and certain knowledge in several parts of this stupendous machine, than
hitherto we could have expected. And though there are
very few that have mathematics enough to understand
his demonstrations; yet the most accurate mathematicians,
who have examined them, allowing them to be such, his
book will deserve to be read, and give no small light and
pleasure to those, who, willing to understand the motions, properties, and operations of the great masses of

[24] Sir Isaac Newton (1642–1727) was "incomparable," not only to
Locke, but to all educated men late in the seventeenth and through-
out the eighteenth centuries; when Voltaire referred to him in 1733
as the greatest man who had ever lived, no one disagreed with him.
He was still "Mr." when Locke wrote these lines, since he was not
knighted until 1705. His "admirable" *Principia* appeared in 1687.—
P. G.

matter in this our solar system, will but carefully mind his conclusions, which may be depended on as propositions well proved.

§ 195. This is, in short, what I have thought concerning a young gentleman's studies; wherein it will possibly be wondered, that I should omit Greek, since amongst the Grecians is to be found the original, as it were, and foundation of all that learning which we have in this part of the world. I grant it so; and will add, that no man can pass for a scholar that is ignorant of the Greek tongue. But I am not here considering the education of a professed scholar, but of a gentleman, to whom Latin and French, as the world now goes, is by every one acknowledged to be necessary. When he comes to be a man, if he has a mind to carry his studies farther, and look into the Greek learning, he will then easily get that tongue himself; and if he has not that inclination, his learning of it under a tutor, will be but lost labour, and much of his time and pains spent in that, which will be neglected and thrown away as soon as he is at liberty. For how many are there of an hundred, even amongst scholars themselves, who retain the Greek they carried from school; or ever improve it to a familiar reading, and perfect understanding of Greek authors?

To conclude this part, which concerns a young gentleman's studies; his tutor should remember, that his business is not so much to teach him all that is knowable, as to raise in him a love and esteem of knowledge; and to put him in the right way of knowing and improving himself, when he has a mind to it.

§ 196. Besides what is to be had from study and books, there are other accomplishments necessary for a gentleman, to be got by exercise, and to which time is to be allowed, and for which masters must be had.

Dancing being that which gives graceful motions all the life, and above all things, manliness and a becoming confidence to young children, I think it cannot be learned too early, after they are once of an age and strength capable of it. But you must be sure to have a good master, that knows, and can teach, what is graceful and becoming, and what gives a freedom and easiness to all the motions of the body. One that teaches not this, is worse than none at all; natural unfashionableness being much better than apish, affected postures; and I think it much more passable to put off the hat, and make a leg, like an honest country gentleman, than like an ill-fashioned dancing-master. For, as for the jigging part, and the figures of dances, I count that little or nothing, farther than as it tends to perfect graceful carriage.

§ 197. Music is thought to have some affinity with dancing, and a good hand, upon some instruments, is by many people mightily valued. But it wastes so much of a young man's time, to gain but a moderate skill in it, and engages often in such odd company, that many think it much better spared: and I have, amongst men of parts and business, so seldom heard any one commended or esteemed for having an excellency in music, that amongst all those things, that ever came into the list of accomplishments, I think I may give it the last place. Our short lives will not serve us for the attainment of all things; nor can our minds be always intent on something to be learned. The weakness of our constitutions, both of mind and body, requires that we should be often unbent: and he that will make a good use of any part of his life, must allow a large portion of it to recreation. At least this must not be denied to young people, unless, whilst you with too much haste make them old, you have the displeasure to set them in their graves, or a second childhood, sooner than you could wish. And therefore I think, that the time and pains allotted to serious improvements should be employed about things of most use and consequence, and that too in the methods the most easy and short that could be at any rate obtained; and perhaps, as I have above said, it would be none of the least secrets of education, to make the exercises in the body and the mind the recreation one to another. I doubt not but that something might be done in it, by a prudent man, that would well consider the temper and inclination of his pupil. For he that is wearied, either with study or dancing, does not desire presently to go to sleep; but to do something else which may divert and delight him. But this must be always remembered, that nothing can come into the account of recreation that is not done with delight.

§ 198. Fencing, and riding the great horse, are looked upon as so necessary parts of breeding, that it would be thought a great omission to neglect them: the latter of the two being for the most part to be learned only in great towns, is one of the best exercises for health which is to be had in those places of ease and luxury; and, upon that account, makes a fit part of a young gentleman's employment, during his abode there. And, as far as it conduces to give a man a firm and graceful seat on horseback, and to make him able to teach his horse to stop, and turn quick, and to rest on his haunches, is of use to a gentleman, both in peace and war. But, whether it be of moment enough to be made a business of, and deserve to take up more of his time than should barely for his health be employed, at due intervals, in some such vigorous exercise, I shall leave to the discretion of parents and tutors; who will do well to remember, in all the parts of education, that most time and application is to be bestowed on that which is like to be of greatest consequence, and frequentest use, in the ordinary course and occurrences of that life the young man is designed for.

§ 199. As for fencing, it seems to me a good exercise for health, but dangerous to the life, the confidence of their skill being apt to engage in quarrels those that think they have learned to use their swords. This presumption makes them often more touchy than needs, on points of honour, and slight or no provocations. But since fencing and riding the great-horse are so generally looked upon as necessary qualifications in the breeding of a gentleman, it will be hard wholly to deny any one of that rank these marks of distinction. I shall leave it therefore to the father, to consider, how far the temper of his son, and the station he is like to be in, will allow or encourage him to comply with fashions, which, having very little to do with civil life, were yet formerly unknown to the most warlike nations; and seem to have added little of force or courage to those who have received them: unless we will think martial skill or prowess have been improved by duelling, with which fencing came into, and with which, I presume, it will go out of the world.

§ 200. These are my present thoughts concerning learning and accomplishments. The great business of all is virtue and wisdom.

"Nullum numen abest, si sit prudentia." [25]

Teach him to get a mastery over his inclinations, and submit his appetite to reason. This being obtained, and by a constant practice settled into habit, the hardest part of the task is over. To bring a young man to this, I know nothing which so much contributes, as the love of praise and commendation, which should therefore be instilled

[25] "If there is good sense, no heavenly power is lacking" (Juvenal *Satires* x. 365).—P. G.

into him by all arts imaginable. Make his mind as sensible of credit and shame as may be: and when you have done that, you have put a principle into him, which will influence his actions, when you are not by; to which the fear of a little smart of a rod is not comparable; and which will be the proper stock whereon afterwards to graft the true principles of morality and religion.

§ 201. I have one thing more to add, which as soon as I mention, I shall run the danger of being suspected to have forgot what I am about, and what I have above written concerning education, all tending towards a gentleman's calling, with which a trade seems wholly to be inconsistent. And yet, I cannot forbear to say, I would have him learn a trade, a manual trade; nay, two or three, but one more particularly.

§ 202. The busy inclination of children being always to be directed to something that may be useful to them, the advantages proposed from what they are set about may be considered of two kinds: 1. Where the skill itself, that is got by exercise, is worth the having. Thus skill not only in languages, and learned sciences, but in painting, turning, gardening, tempering and working in iron, and all other useful arts, is worth the having. 2. Where the exercise itself, without any consideration, is necessary or useful for health. Knowledge in some things is so necessary to be got by children, whilst they are young, that some part of their time is to be allotted to their improvement in them, though those employments contribute nothing at all to their health: such are reading, and writing, and all other sedentary studies, for the cultivating of the mind, which unavoidably take up a great part of gentlemen's time, quite from their cradles. Other manual arts, which are both got and exercised by labour, do many of them, by that exercise, not only increase our dexterity and skill, but contribute to our health too; especially such as employ us in the open air. In these, then, health and improvement may be joined together; and of these should some fit ones be chosen, to be made the recreations of one, whose chief business is with books and study. In this choice, the age and inclination of the person is to be considered, and constraint always to be avoided in bringing him to it. For command and force may often create, but can never cure an aversion; and whatever any one is brought to by compulsion, he will leave as soon as he can, and be little profited and less recreated by, whilst he is at it.

§ 203.   That which of all others would please me best would be a painter, were there not an argument or two against it, not easy to be answered. First, ill painting is one of the worst things in the world; and to attain a tolerable degree of skill in it requires too much of a man's time. If he has a natural inclination to it, it will endanger the neglect of all other more useful studies, to give way to that; and if he have no inclination to it, all the time, pains, and money shall be employed in it will be thrown away to no purpose. Another reason why I am not for painting in a gentleman, is, because it is a sedentary recreation, which more employs the mind than the body. A gentleman's more serious employment, I look on to be study; and when that demands relaxation and refreshment, it should be in some exercise of the body, which unbends the thought, and confirms the health and strength. For these two reasons I am not for painting.

§ 204.   In the next place, for a country gentleman, I should propose one, or rather both these; viz. gardening or husbandry in general, and working in wood, as a carpenter, joiner, or turner; these being fit and healthy recreations for a man of study or business.

§ 206.   Nor let it be thought, that I mistake, when I call these or the like exercises of manual arts, diversions or recreations; for recreation is not being idle, (as every one may observe) but easing the wearied part by change of business: and he that thinks diversion may not lie in hard and painful labour, forgets the early rising, hard riding, heat, cold and hunger of huntsmen, which is yet known to be the constant recreation of men of the greatest condition. Delving, planting, inoculating, or any the like profitable employments, would be no less a diversion, than any of the idle sports in fashion, if men could but be brought to delight in them, which custom and skill in a trade will quickly bring any one to do. And I doubt not but there are to be found those, who, being frequently called to cards, or any other play, by those they could not refuse, have been more tired with these recreations than with any the most serious employment of life: though the play has been such as they have naturally had no aversion to, and with which they could willingly sometimes divert themselves.

§ 207.   Play, wherein persons of condition, especially ladies, waste so much of their time, is a plain instance to me, that men cannot be perfectly idle; they must be doing something. For how else could they sit so many hours toiling at that, which generally gives more vexation than delight to people, whilst they are actually engaged in it? It is certain, gaming leaves no satisfaction behind it to those who reflect when it is over; and it no way profits either body or mind: as to their estates, if it strike so deep as to concern them, it is a trade then, and not a recreation, wherein few, that have any thing else to live on, thrive; and, at best, a thriving gamester has but a poor trade on it, who fills his pockets at the price of his reputation.

Recreation belongs not to people who are strangers to business, and are not wasted and wearied with the employment of their calling. The skill should be, so to order their time of recreation, that it may relax and refresh the part that has been exercised, and is tired; and yet do something, which, besides the present delight and ease, may produce what will afterwards be profitable. It has been nothing but the vanity and pride of greatness and riches, that has brought unprofitable and dangerous pastimes (as they are called) into fashion, and persuaded people into a belief, that the learning or putting their hands to any thing that was useful, could not be a diversion fit for a gentleman. This has been that which has given cards, dice, and drinking, so much credit in the world; and a great many throw away their spare hours in them, through the prevalency of custom, and want of some better employment to fill up the vacancy of leisure, more than from any real delight is to be found in them. They cannot bear the dead weight of unemployed time lying upon their hands, nor the uneasiness it is to do nothing at all; and having never learned any laudable manual art, wherewith to divert themselves, they have recourse to those foolish or ill ways in use, to help off their time, which a rational man, till corrupted by custom, could find very little pleasure in.

§ 208. I say not this, that I would never have a young gentleman accommodate himself to the innocent diversions in fashion, amongst those of his age and condition. I am so far from having him austere and morose to that degree, that I would persuade him to more than ordinary complaisance for all the gaieties and diversions of those he converses with, and be averse or testy in nothing they should desire of him, that might become a gentleman, and an honest man: though, as to cards and dice, I think the safest and best way is never to learn any play upon them, and so to be incapacitated for those dangerous temptations, and incroaching wasters of useful time. But allowance being made for idle and jovial conversation, and all fashionable becoming recreations; I say, a young man will have time enough, from his serious and main business, to learn almost any trade. It is for want of application, and not of leisure, that men are not skilful in more arts than one; and an hour in a day constantly employed in such a way of diversion, will carry a man in a short time a great deal farther than he can imagine: which, if it were of no other use but to drive the common, vicious, useless, and dangerous pastimes out of fashion, and to show there was no need of them, would deserve to be encouraged. If men from their youth were weaned from that sauntering humour, wherein some, out of custom, let a good part of their lives run uselessly away, without either business or recreation; they would find time enough to acquire dexterity and skill in hundreds of things, which, though remote from their proper callings, would not at all interfere with them. And therefore, I think, for this, as well as other reasons before-mentioned, a lazy, listless humour, that idly dreams away the days, is of all others the least to be indulged, or permitted in young people. It is the proper state of one sick, and out of order in his health, and is tolerable in nobody else, of what age or condition soever.

§ 209. To the arts abovementioned may be added perfuming, varnishing, graving, and several sorts of working in iron, brass, and silver: and if, as it happens to most young gentlemen, that a considerable part of his time be spent in a great town, he may learn to cut, polish, and set precious stones, or employ himself in grinding and polishing optical glasses. Amongst the great variety

there is of ingenious manual arts, it will be impossible
that no one should be found to please and delight him,
unless he be either idle or debauched, which is not to be
supposed in a right way of education. And since he cannot be always employed in study, reading, and conversation, there will be many an hour, besides what his exercises will take up, which, if not spent this way, will be
spent worse. For, I conclude, a young man will seldom
desire to sit perfectly still and idle; or if he does, it is a
fault that ought to be mended.

§ 210.   But if his mistaken parents, frightened with
the disgraceful names of mechanic and trade, shall have
an aversion to any thing of this kind in their children;
yet there is one thing relating to trade, which, when they
consider, they will think absolutely necessary for their
sons to learn.

Merchants' accounts, though a science not likely to help
a gentleman to get an estate, yet possibly there is not any
thing of more use and efficacy to make him preserve the
estate he has. It is seldom observed, that he who keeps
an account of his income and expenses, and thereby has
constantly under view the course of his domestic affairs,
lets them run to ruin; and I doubt not but many a man
gets behind-hand, before he is aware, or runs further on,
when he is once in, for want of this care, or the skill to
do it. I would therefore advise all gentlemen to learn
perfectly merchants' accounts, and not to think it is a
skill that belongs not to them, because it has received its
name from, and has been chiefly practised by, men of
traffic.

§ 211.   When my young master has once got the skill
of keeping accounts (which is a business of reason more
than arithmetic), perhaps it will not be amiss, that his
father from thenceforth require him to do it in all his

concernments. Not that I would have him set down every pint of wine, or play, that costs him money; the general name of expenses will serve for such things well enough: nor would I have his father look so narrowly into these accounts, as to take occasion from thence to criticise on his expenses. He must remember, that he himself was once a young man, and not forget the thoughts he had then, nor the right his son has to have the same, and to have allowance made for them. If therefore I would have the young gentleman obliged to keep an account, it is not at all to have that way a check upon his expenses, (for what the father allows him, he ought to let him be fully master of), but only, that he might be brought early into the custom of doing it, and that it might be made familiar and habitual to him betimes, which will be so useful and necessary to be constantly practised through the whole course of his life. A noble Venetian, whose son wallowed in the plenty of his father's riches, finding his son's expenses grow very high and extravagant, ordered his cashier to let him have, for the future, no more money than what he should count when he received it. This one would think no great restraint to a young gentleman's expenses, who could freely have as much money as he would tell. But yet this, to one, who was used to nothing but the pursuit of his pleasures, proved a very great trouble, which at last ended in this sober and advantageous reflection: "If it be so much pains to me, barely to count the money I would spend; what labour and pains did it cost my ancestors, not only to count, but get it?" This rational thought, suggested by this little pains imposed upon him, wrought so effectually upon his mind, that it made him take up, and from that time forwards prove a good husband. This at least every body must allow, that nothing is likelier to keep a man within compass, than the having constantly before his eyes the state of his affairs, in a regular course of account.

§ 212. The last part, usually, in education, is travel, which is commonly thought to finish the work, and complete the gentleman. I confess, travel into foreign countries has great advantages; but the time usually chosen to send young men abroad, is, I think, of all other, that which renders them least capable of reaping those advantages. Those which are proposed, as to the main of them, may be reduced to these two: first, language; secondly, an improvement in wisdom and prudence, by seeing men, and conversing with people of tempers, customs, and ways of living, different from one another, and especially from those of his parish and neighbourhood. But from sixteen to one-and-twenty, which is the ordinary time of travel, men are, of all their lives, the least suited to these improvements. The first season to get foreign languages, and form the tongue to their true accents, I should think, should be from seven to fourteen or sixteen; and then, too, a tutor with them is useful and necessary, who may, with those languages, teach them other things. But to put them out of their parents' view, at a great distance, under a governor, when they think themselves too much men to be governed by others, and yet have not prudence and experience enough to govern themselves: what is it but to expose them to all the greatest dangers of their whole life, when they have the least fence and guard against them? Till that boiling boisterous part of life comes on, it may be hoped the tutor may have some authority; neither the stubbornness of age, nor the temptation or examples of others, can take him from his tutor's conduct, till fifteen or sixteen: but then, when he begins to consort himself with men, and thinks himself one; when he comes to relish, and pride himself in, manly vices, and thinks it a shame to be any longer under the control and conduct of another: what can be hoped from even the most careful and discreet governor, when neither he has power to compel, nor his pupil a disposition to be persuaded; but, on the contrary, has the advice of warm blood, and prevailing fashion, to hearken to the temptations of his companions, just as wise as himself, rather than to the persuasions of his tutor, who is now looked on as the enemy to his freedom? And when is a man so like to miscarry, as when at the same time he is both raw and unruly? This is the season of all his life that most requires the eye and authority of his parents and friends, to govern it. The flexibleness of the former part of a man's age, not yet grown up to be headstrong, makes it more governable and safe; and, in the after-part, reason and foresight begin a little to take place, and mind a man of his safety and improvement. The time, therefore, I should think the fittest for a young gentleman to be sent abroad, would be, either when he is younger, under a tutor, whom he might be the better for; or when he is some years older, without a governor; when he is of age to govern himself, and make observations of what he finds in other countries worthy his notice, and that might be of use to him after his return: and when too, being thoroughly acquainted with the laws and fashions, the natural and moral advantages and defects of his own country, he has something to exchange with those abroad, from whose conversation he hoped to reap any knowledge.

§ 213. The ordering of travel otherwise, is that, I imagine, which makes so many young gentlemen come back so little improved by it. And if they do bring home with them any knowledge of the places and people they have seen, it is often an admiration of the worst and vainest practices they met with abroad; retaining a relish and memory of those things, wherein their liberty took its first swing, rather than of what should make them better and wiser after their return. And, indeed, how can it be otherwise, going abroad at the age they do, under the care of another, who is to provide their necessaries, and make their observations for them? Thus under the shelter and pretence of a governor, thinking themselves excused from standing upon their own legs, or being accountable for their own conduct, they very seldom trouble themselves with inquiries, or making useful observations of their own. Their thoughts run after play and pleasure, wherein they take it as a lessening to be controlled: but seldom trouble themselves to examine the designs, observe the address, and consider the arts, tempers, and inclinations of men they meet with; that so they may know how to comport themselves towards them. Here he that travels with them, is to skreen them, get them out, when they have run themselves into the briars; and in all their miscarriages be answerable for them.

§ 214. I confess, the knowledge of men is so great a skill, that it is not to be expected a young man should presently be perfect in it. But yet his going abroad is to little purpose, if travel does not sometimes open his eyes, make him cautious and wary, and accustom him to look beyond the outside, and, under the inoffensive guard of a civil and obliging carriage, keep himself free and safe in his conversation with strangers, and all sorts of people, without forfeiting their good opinion. He that is sent out to travel at the age, and with the thoughts, of a man designing to improve himself, may get into the conversation and acquaintance of persons of condition where he comes: which, though a thing of most advantage to a gentleman that travels, yet, I ask, amongst our young men that go abroad under tutors, what one is there of a hundred that ever visits any person of quality? much less makes an acquaintance with such, from whose conversation he may learn what is good breeding in that country, and what is worth observation in it; though from such persons it is, one may learn more in one day than in a year's rambling from one inn to another. Nor indeed is it to be wondered; for men of worth and parts will not easily admit the familiarity of boys, who yet need the care of a tutor; though a young gentleman and stranger, appearing like a man, and showing a desire to inform himself in the customs, manners, laws, and government of the country he is in, will find welcome assistance and entertainment amongst the best and most knowing persons every where, who will be ready to receive, encourage, and countenance any ingenious and inquisitive foreigner.

§ 215. This, how true soever it be, will not, I fear, alter the custom, which has cast the time of travel upon the worst part of a man's life; but for reasons not taken from their improvement. The young lad must not be ventured abroad at eight or ten, for fear of what may happen to the tender child, though he then runs ten times less risk than at sixteen or eighteen. Nor must he stay at home till that dangerous heady age be over, because he must be back again by one-and-twenty, to marry and propagate. The father cannot stay any longer for the portion, nor the mother for a new set of babies to play with: and so my young master, whatever comes on it, must have a wife looked out for him, by that time he is of age; though it would be no prejudice to his strength, his parts, or his issue, if it were respited for some time, and he had leave to get, in years and knowledge, the start a little of his children, who are often found to tread too near upon the heels of their fathers, to the no great satisfaction either of son or father. But the young gentleman being got within view of matrimony, it is time to leave him to his mistress.

§ 216. Though I am now come to a conclusion of what obvious remarks have suggested to me concerning education, I would not have it thought, that I look on it as a just treatise on this subject. There are a thousand other things that may need consideration; especially if one should take in the various tempers, different inclinations, and particular defaults, that are to be found in children; and prescribe proper remedies. The variety is so great, that it would require a volume; nor would that reach it. Each man's mind has some peculiarity, as well as his face, that distinguishes him from all others; and there are possibly scarce two children, who can be conducted by exactly the same method. Besides that, I think a prince, a nobleman, and an ordinary gentleman's son, should have different ways of breeding. But having had here only some general views, in reference to the main end and aims in education, and those designed for a gentleman's son, whom, being then very little, I considered only as white paper, or wax, to be moulded and fashioned as one pleases; I have touched little more than those heads, which I judged necessary for the breeding of a young gentleman of his condition in general; and have now published these my occasional thoughts, with this hope, that, though this be far from being a complete treatise on this subject, or such as that every one may find what will just fit his child in it; yet it may give some small light to those, whose concern for their dear little ones makes them so irregularly bold, that they dare venture to consult their own reason, in the education of their children, rather than wholly to rely upon old custom.

PETER GAY, Professor of History at Columbia University, was born in Berlin, Germany, in 1923. He received his B.A. from the University of Denver. After receiving his M.A. and Ph.D. from Columbia University, he taught government there from 1947 until 1955, when he joined the university's Department of History. Professor Gay's writings include *The Dilemma of Democratic Socialism: Edward Bernstein's Challenge to Marx* (1952), *Voltaire's Politics: The Poet as Realist* (1959), and *The Party of Humanity: Essays in the French Enlightenment* (1964), in addition to translations of works by Voltaire and Ernst Cassirer.